BOOK ONE (K–6)

Exploring Statistics in the Elementary Grades

Developed by teachers for teachers

Carolyn Bereska
Teacher, writer
Baltimore County Public Schools

Cyrilla H. Bolster
Teacher, writer
Baltimore County Public Schools

L. Carey Bolster
Project Director, K–12 Math Projects
PBS MATHLINE

Dr. Richard Scheaffer
Statistics Department
University of Florida

D1502390

DALE SEYMOUR PUBLICATIONS®
White Plains, New York

The Elementary Quantitative Literacy (EQL) project was prepared under the auspices of the American Statistical Association and was funded in part by ASA and by the National Science Foundation Grant No. 9053572

This project was supported, in part,
by the
National Science Foundation
Opinions expressed are those of the authors
and not necessarily those of the Foundation

Co-principal Investigators: Cyrilla H. Bolster, Richard Scheaffer
Curriculum Development: Carolyn Bereska, L. Carey Bolster
Managing Editor: Catherine Anderson
Project Editor: Ellen Harding
Production/Manufacturing Director: Janet Yearian
Production/Manufacturing Coordinator: Claire Flaherty
Design Manager: Jeff Kelly
Text design: Carolyn Deacy
Cover design: Ray Godfrey
Illustrations: Rachel Gage
Composition: Claire Flaherty

This book is published by Dale Seymour Publications®, an imprint of Addison Wesley Longman, Inc.
Dale Seymour Publications
10 Bank Street
White Plains, NY 10602
Customer Service: 800-872-1100

Order number 21830
ISBN 1-57232-344-2

3 4 5 6 7 8 9 10-ML-01 00

CONTENTS

ABOUT EQL

Are you an elementary classroom teacher?

Have you had limited experience with statistics and probability?

Do you wish you knew more statistics and statistical language so you could enhance your students' understanding?

Do you wish a statistician could provide the statistical language for the lessons you teach?

If you answered yes to any of these questions, we had you in mind when we designed this book.

The people developing this project are classroom teachers with many years of experience. We were fortunate to have statisticians work with us as we developed these lessons. They provided precise ways to express both vocabulary and symbolism, and guided us as we developed high-interest, high-content statistics lessons at the elementary level.

Statisticians and college pre-service instructors worked with us to develop the scope and sequence. One-week workshops were presented in a variety of states to field-test the

materials. The result of the field-test was the basis for the revision of these materials; they then became the cornerstone of Elementary Quantitative Literacy (EQL).

There are lesson ideas in these books that you may already be using. Our goal is to present developmentally appropriate activities that are interesting and engaging, introduce concepts, develop notions and statistical vocabulary, and serve as a resource to you, the teacher. It is our hope teachers will become so familiar with the process of investigating a statistical question, they will look for statistical opportunities in the classroom and create unique lesson plans that complement the curricula being taught. We created this program to serve as a guide that supplies the reference information, statistical lesson outlines, and a glossary of terms. We hope EQL will enable you to create many, many more learning opportunities.

The EQL Team

INFORMATION ABOUT THE EQL PROGRAM

Exploring Statistics in the Elementary Grades, Book 1 is the Introductory Level of this two-part program. This first book presents activities for elementary students (K–6) by providing a foundation in quantitative literacy. Activities are engaging while building statistical concepts in a developmental sequence and introducing and using vocabulary specific to statistics and probability. The activities focus on finding meaningful patterns in data and possible associations between data sets by both graphical (line plot, stem and leaf plot, and scatter plot) and numerical (percent, median, and mean) techniques.

Exploring Statistics in the Elementary Grades, Book 2 is the Intermediate Level of this program. The emphasis on finding patterns and associations in data sets is carried to a deeper level of understanding for students in grades 3–8. The techniques of Book 1 are used in more complex situations and this book includes new graphical (box plot, time series plot, and two-way frequency tables) and numerical (quartiles and interquartile range) techniques.

All lessons have been field tested over a period of several years with different age groups and different geographic populations. Depending on the developmental stage of the students, the lessons are designed to be used with early primary through late intermediate level students. Adaptations to individual lesson plans have been made to accommodate the developmental readiness of the students and are labeled: For the Primary Student and For the Intermediate Student. Lessons without these labels mean that the lesson is appropriate for both primary and intermediate students without a major adaptation.

Early primary students may need more time to develop an idea. Also they may need spin-off lessons that reinforce the lesson objective and statistical terms. Intermediate students may enjoy a greater amount of decision making with larger portions of the lesson devoted to student discourse and student/teacher dialogue.

The vocabulary and statistical concepts are defined and illustrated in a teacher-friendly format and cross-referenced to the Ready Reference pages and the Glossary. The materials are written to enhance the content background of the teacher and to provide actual lessons to be adapted for the students.

Once the lesson is taught, the same lesson outline can be used with real data from science class, social studies, or math class. This provides lesson integration (cross curricular) and greater understanding, ownership, and participation in quantitative literacy.

Investigation Overview

Three important pieces of information are summarized here for you. Statistical Ideas lists the concepts to be covered in the lesson. Materials/Resources alerts you to the needed preparations and the appropriate Ready Reference materials. Understanding the Problem gives you help in setting up the problem for your class.

The Student Transparency

Duplicate this blackline page on an overhead transparency to display at the beginning of the lesson. Its purpose is to pose an opening question (presenting the problem) that will lead to class discussion of ways to solve the problem. Always allow students to read and react to the problem before distributing the worksheets.

Teaching the Investigation

The lesson format is provided by the American Statistical Association in the publication "Guidelines for the Teaching of Statistics K–12."

- Presenting the question
- Understanding the problem
- Gathering and organizing data
- Describing and interpreting the data
- Drawing conclusions
- Additional investigations and projects

The purpose for teaching this outline is to build the structure a student should follow when conducting his or her own investigations. Each lesson follows these distinct steps for the investigation. Through repeated use of these subsections in a lesson plan, a sequence of steps should become automatic to the student. Ready Reference 1 focuses thinking about this sequence. Leading questions for the teacher are included on this reference page that may assist the teacher in focusing thinking and class discussion to the specific phase of the investigation.

Ready Reference Pages

Ready Reference pages define the data display, pose a problem in which the data display would be appropriate, and give a step-by-step illustrated sequence for how to construct the display. The pages may be duplicated for classroom use. They can be laminated or placed in plastic page protectors and kept with other classroom reference materials for use in future investigations.

Glossary

Appropriate statistical terms are introduced throughout the lessons in a sequence that will build a complete statistical vocabulary for the teacher and students. At the back of this book a glossary of terms is presented alphabetically for quick reference. Definitions of the terms used in each Lesson can be posted in the classroom to build and develop statistical vocabulary.

ACKNOWLEDGMENTS

We would like to offer our thanks and appreciation to the following people who assisted in the preparation of this book.

The classroom teachers who assisted in the preparation of materials, participated in field-testing lessons, and helped to make the EQL workshops a reality that became nationwide:

Delores Berry, Kathleen Dengler, Leona Lee, Kathy Shell, Sally Smith, and Sara Turnipseed

The classroom teachers who enthusiastically participated in EQL workshops, and subsequently became presenters of EQL workshops:

Kathi Bletz, JoAnn Carson, Laura Cleveland, Nancy Dryden, Jennifer Ebmeier, Linda Gosson, Dee Hobrle, Sharon Hopkins, Ron Kussrow, Kristen Massa, Debbie Oldendick, Ellen Pyles, and Paulette Williams

Mathematics teachers at the middle and high school level who offered their expertise to our elementary project:

Jim Heiser, Leo Karageorge, Jackie Lamp, Paul Leimbach, and Karen Taylor

Special thanks to Pat Marston for preparing the initial materials.

The many statisticians who offered their guidance, suggestions, reactions, instructions, and support:

Jackie Benedetti, Barry Bodt, Malcolm Taylor, June Morita, Nancy Temkin, Cheryl Olszewski, Ellen Wijsman, Linda Young, and all the staff of the American Statistical Association: Barbara Bailor, Cathy Crocker, Kathryn B. Rowe, and Ray Waller

The EQL project advisory staff:

Ann Beyer, Barry Bodt, Elizabeth Eltinge, Martin Johnson, Mary Lindquist, Susan Jo Russell, and Malcolm Taylor

The many students in elementary schools from Nebraska, South Carolina, Iowa, Washington, Maryland, and New Hampshire who were taught using the Elementary Quantitative Literacy lessons

Ice Cream Preferences

INVESTIGATION OVERVIEW

Statistical Ideas

- Establishing the need and value for graphing information
- Experiencing the differences in reading information in contrast with interpreting a graph

Materials/Resources

- Blackline Master 1, **Ice Cream Sundae Survey** (paragraph form), page 6 (one for each student in one half of the class)
- Blackline Master 2, **Ice Cream Sundae Survey** (graph form), page 7 (one for each student in the other half of the class)
- Ready Reference 1, **A Problem-Solving Approach to Investigating Data**, page 120

Understanding the Problem

Display the student transparency. Allow students to read and react to the problem. Distribute the worksheets face down.

Give students on the left side of the room the paragraph form of the worksheet and students on the right side of the room the graph form of the same survey. Don't tell students that there are two different worksheets. Putting a time limit on the activity focuses each student on the activity.

Can You Answer Questions from an Ice Cream Sundae Survey?

In a survey, students were asked to name the ice cream flavors they liked best. This information is on a worksheet that has been placed face down in front of you.

When you are given the signal, turn the paper over and read the survey results.

You will have 10 seconds to read the survey. Then you will be asked some questions about it.

Can you tell what you've learned from the survey?

TEACHING THE INVESTIGATION

Gathering Information

Asking the following questions in rapid-fire format will help you get responses quickly, as well as keep the students focused on reading and searching for the information.

➤ How many students chose plain vanilla ice cream? [2]

➤ How many students chose chocolate and vanilla? [4]

➤ Which student liked chocolate and strawberry? [Kara]

At this point, remark that the answers seem to be coming from all the students on the same side of the room. Continue to ask questions:

➤ How many students liked chocolate and strawberry? [1]

➤ How many students liked vanilla and strawberry? [2]

➤ Which flavor combination was the most popular? [chocolate and vanilla]

Continue to remark:

"Gosh, this one side of the room is really quick today," or, "I hope to hear from this side of the room on the next answer," and so on.

Continue asking questions, unless there is a vast amount of frustration. Decide when to halt the questioning.

Additional question suggestions:

➤ How many students responded to this survey? [12]

➤ How many students preferred chocolate-chip cookie dough? [2]

Describing and Interpreting the Data

Decide when to tell the group that they have different worksheets. A remark such as, "Does it seem to you that the students sitting on this side of the room seem to be answering these questions very quickly?" "Does it make you wonder how they are able to locate the information so quickly?"

Instruct the students to hold up the worksheet they used (the graph) that allowed them to answer the questions so quickly. Now instruct the other group to show their worksheets. Give the students a chance to react.

Drawing Conclusions

Encourage students to make statements about their feelings, either frustrations or successes.

Elicit from the students that a table or graph has the following advantages:

- Organizes the material
- Allows easy readability
- Increases the speed of response
- Allows quick comparison
- Enables the reader to rank highest, lowest, and equal responses

Graphs are visual displays that can be used to interpret data rapidly.

The purpose of this activity is to establish the need and value for graphing techniques, to motivate students to learn more, and to show the power of mathematics.

Additional Investigations and Projects

➤ Name situations in daily life where information is coded for quick interpretation. [area codes in a phone number, zip codes on letters, road signs, social security numbers, precautions on a prescription bottle, icons on a computer menu, and so on]

➤ Have students write an activity similar to the one presented and construct a graph with the same information. Supply a list of written questions. Set a timer and see how long it takes two people to answer the questions. Compare their times.

➤ You may want to use this activity on Parent Night as an introduction to the probability and statistics strand in the mathematics program.

Ice Cream Sundae Survey

Lauren liked chocolate and vanilla. Kyle liked plain vanilla. Oliver also liked plain vanilla. Meka and Zac liked chocolate-chip cookie dough. Oh, I forgot to mention that Lilly, Isabel, and Sam also liked chocolate and vanilla. Kara chose chocolate and strawberry. Mariko liked plain strawberry and Bryan and Ty chose vanilla and strawberry.

Ice Cream Sundae Survey

Ice Cream Sundaes

			Isabel		
			Lilly		
Zac	Oliver		Sam		Ty
Meka	Kyle	Mariko	Lauren	Kara	Bryan
Chocolate-Chip Cookie Dough	Plain Vanilla	Plain Straw-berry	Chocolate and Vanilla	Chocolate and Straw-berry	Vanilla and Straw-berry

EQL INVESTIGATION 2

Vary, Vary Interesting Things

INVESTIGATION OVERVIEW

Statistical Ideas

- Classifying materials according to one **attribute** or **variable**
- Discovering which attributes produce interesting results

Materials/Resources

- Bundles of a wide variety of materials, such as wallpaper samples, buttons, fabric swatches, alphabet letters, attribute blocks, catalog pictures of tools, jewelry, or hats (one bundle per group of 3 or 4).
- Chart paper and markers
- Ready Reference 1, **A Problem-Solving Approach to Investigating Data**, page 120

Understanding the Problem

Display the student transparency. Allow students to read and react to the problem. Distribute the worksheets face down.

Use these questions to facilitate discussion. They will help students organize their thoughts as they analyze the problem. You may also use questions from Ready Reference 1, page 120.

➤ What is in the bag or bundle? How might you sort it?

➤ Consider different possibilities for sorting your materials.

➤ Consider how you will represent your groupings on chart paper.

How Would You Sort these Materials?

It's always interesting to see how other people organize things. You will be working in small groups and analyzing materials in a bag or bundle. How can these materials be sorted? Are there several ways these materials can be sorted?

Gathering and Organizing the Data

Have students work in small groups of 3 or 4. Give each group a bag or bundle of materials. Ask group members to discuss possible ways to sort or categorize the materials. Students in each group should choose one attribute to be their **sorting factor**. This attribute may result in different outcomes. For example, sorting by color may yield different results from sorting by size.

Have students organize the objects according to the attribute they chose. An example is shown below for sorting buttons by color. Students tend to sort first by a more obvious characteristic. Discussion within each group can lead to discovering subtle attributes that may have gone unnoticed.

For Primary Students:

Allow students to explore and discuss the objects as they sort them. Have each group report the information to you. Then you can assist students in using the actual objects to make a physical graph. Groups can invite other groups to view their graphs as they explain them.

For Intermediate Students:

Give students these directions:

Make a first sketch of your display. Select a different attribute and re-sort your materials using this new sorting factor. Make another sketch of your new display.

Sorting Buttons By Color

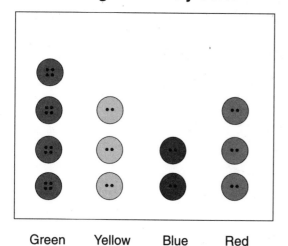

Green   Yellow   Blue   Red

Sorting Buttons By Attachment

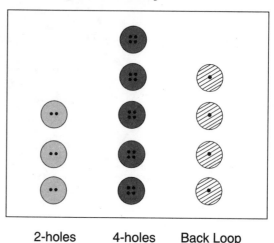

2-holes   4-holes   Back Loop

Sorting Displays These four pages contain examples of the wide variety of objects and the kinds of displays that students have created as they worked on this investigation.

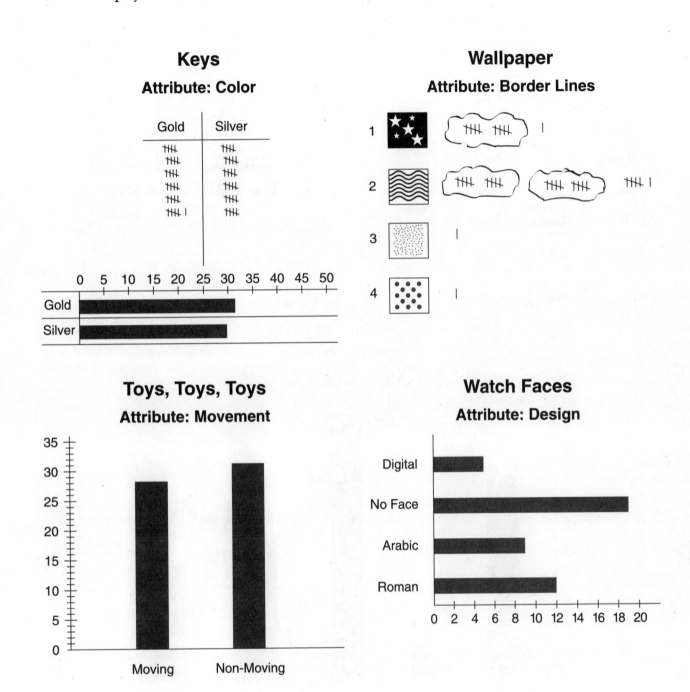

Keys

Attribute: Color

Wallpaper

Attribute: Border Lines

Toys, Toys, Toys

Attribute: Movement

Watch Faces

Attribute: Design

Sorting Displays–*Continued.*

Types of Baseball Caps
Attribute: Design

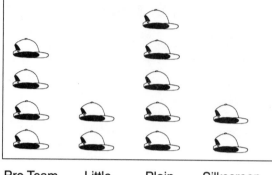

| Pro Team Logo (Patch) | Little League Team Logo (Patch) | Plain | Silkscreen or Painted Design or Logo |

Shells
Attribute: Shape

Whole ▪▪▪▪▫   Broken ▪▪▪▫

Types of Shells
Attribute: Shape

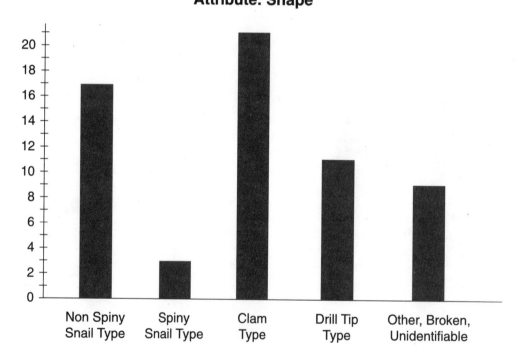

| Non Spiny Snail Type | Spiny Snail Type | Clam Type | Drill Tip Type | Other, Broken, Unidentifiable |

Sorting Displays–*Continued.*

Classification of Sea Shells

Attribute: Type

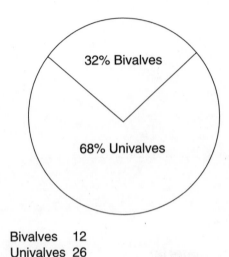

32% Bivalves

68% Univalves

Bivalves   12
Univalves 26

How Many Buttons Are on Our Clothes?

Attribute: Number

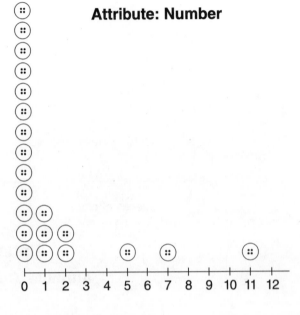

0 1 2 3 4 5 6 7 8 9 10 11 12

Real Pets of Miss Patrick's Class

Attribute: Type

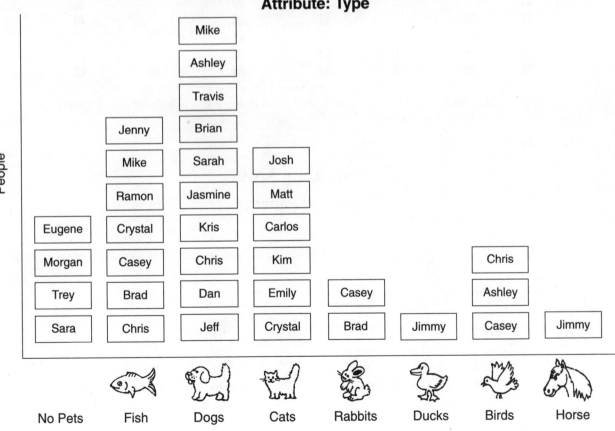

People

No Pets	Fish	Dogs	Cats	Rabbits	Ducks	Birds	Horse
		Mike					
		Ashley					
		Travis					
	Jenny	Brian					
	Mike	Sarah	Josh				
	Ramon	Jasmine	Matt				
Eugene	Crystal	Kris	Carlos				
Morgan	Casey	Chris	Kim			Chris	
Trey	Brad	Dan	Emily	Casey		Ashley	
Sara	Chris	Jeff	Crystal	Brad	Jimmy	Casey	Jimmy

Fabric Squares

Attribute: Texture

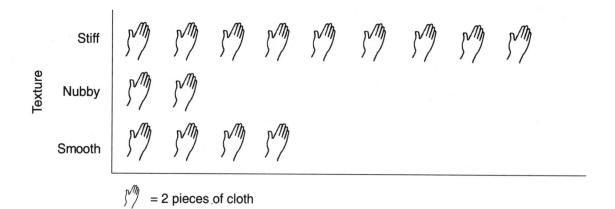

 = 2 pieces of cloth

Alphabet Letters

Attribute: Construction Material

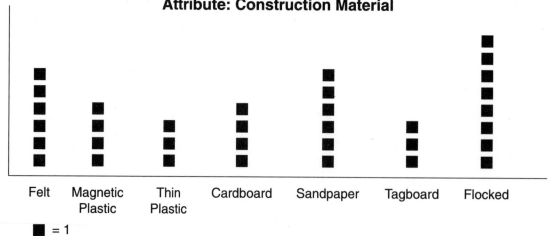

| Felt | Magnetic Plastic | Thin Plastic | Cardboard | Sandpaper | Tagboard | Flocked |

■ = 1

Fabric Squares

Attribute: Patterns

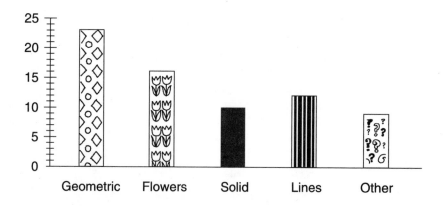

Describing and Interpreting the Data

Have students present their displays to the class. Discuss the following questions.

➤ What sorting factor was used? [Color, use, size, shape, material or construction, and so on.]

➤ How many categories are there using this attribute? [If sorting by color, how many colors are in this collection, and so on?]

➤ Of which object did you have the most? the least? equal amounts?

➤ In what other ways could the materials have been sorted? What made categorizing in this manner interesting? Why did your group choose this method of sorting?

➤ How does sorting your material reveal descriptions you might not have otherwise noticed?

➤ Did any other group present a display that used the same attribute for sorting? If you used the same sorting factor, did your displays look similar?

➤ Are there factors, such as number within a category, that affected how you sorted these objects? [If many items are sorted into a few categories, the count is higher than if many items are sorted into a lot of categories. If the sorting involves only two categories, (blue and not blue), it may be quick and easy but the results may be less interesting than if a larger number of specific categories are created.]

Drawing Conclusions

Have students write a note to one of the groups giving them feedback on their display. In the note, they should use the following questions.

➤ Did they display information in a clever way?

➤ Was there something particularly clear and easy to interpret?

➤ Would you like to make suggestions?

➤ Have you discovered additional ways you could have constructed your graphic display?

Use the graphic displays as a formative assessment piece to focus future direction and discussion of the areas of need, such as: spacing, scaling, proper labeling (title, key, categories), ease of reading, experience with reading bar graphs, or Venn diagrams.

Additional Investigations and Projects

Play Gatekeeper:

All participants hold an attribute block and stand in a line.

Participants file past the gatekeeper, who has one attribute in mind. The participants are admitted with a "yes" if their attribute matches the sorting factor in the mind of the gate keeper (for example, all squares). Others are turned away with a "no" because they don't have the correct sorting factor. The group then identifies the sorting factor used by the gatekeeper.

There may be a second gatekeeper who has a different attribute in mind (for example, all yellow), and the game can continue with those who passed through the first gate. Those who are allowed to pass through the second gate have two common attributes. (In this case, they are both square and yellow.)

This will give an introduction to bivariate data (two measurements) and can provide an introduction to line graphs and scatter plots (graphs with a scale on the x-axis and y-axis simultaneously).

➤ After playing Gatekeeper with two gate-keepers, collect and organize the data from one of these games. Venn diagrams work well when visualizing attribute data.

➤ Use this kind of activity in other subject areas. Classify rocks, leaves, shells, and so on, as an extension of a science topic. Sort letters of the alphabet according to similarity (primary level) or lines of symmetry (intermediate level). Provide a U.S. map to groups. Cut out the states. Organize states according to common attributes as an extension of a social studies topic.

Phony Phone Numbers

INVESTIGATION OVERVIEW

Statistical Ideas

- Making a **line plot**
- Finding the **mode**
- Describing the **distribution** of data: **clusters, gaps, outliers, symmetry, skewness**

Materials/Resources

- Old telephone directory

Per Group:
- Graph paper
- Rulers
- Highlighter or crayon
- Ready Reference 2, **Line Plots**, page 121

Understanding the Problem

Display the student transparency. Allow students to read and react to the problem. Distribute the worksheets face down.

Use these questions to facilitate discussion. They will help students organize their thoughts as they analyze the problem. You may also use questions from Ready Reference 1, page 120.

➤ Can we collect information from a page of the local telephone directory? Will it help us determine the most often used first digit of a telephone number?

➤ Would this sample be the same for the whole area?

➤ Should we take a sample of the page? How could we take a sample? How would you organize the data?

What Number Should Mrs. Bell Call?

Mrs. Bell wants to call her son, Alexander, to ring in the new year. She has a very poor memory, so she looks up his number in her address book, but she can't read the first digit. Mrs. Bell is at a pay phone and has only three quarters. What number do you think she should try as the first digit? What do you think is the most often used first digit in a telephone number?

Gathering and Organizing the Data

For Primary Students:

Ask the children to name all the numbers that are on the telephone. Have students write their phone numbers on a piece of paper and circle the first digit. Create a line plot on the chalkboard and have individual students make an X above the number which is the first digit of his or her telephone number. Self-stick removable notes can be used instead of X's. Discuss the results.

First Digit of Our Phone Numbers

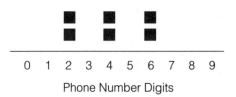

```
0  1  2  3  4  5  6  7  8  9
```
Phone Number Digits

For Intermediate Students:

Have students collect data concerning the first digit of each class member's telephone number. Have students make a line plot of the class data. Ask these questions:

➤ Was there a high number of repeat digits? [Generally, people living in the same neighborhood will have the same exchange.]

➤ Were there any digits that were not used? Why?

Ask: What do you think will happen to the shape of the data on the line plot if the phone numbers are selected from a phone book page?

Form small groups of students and distribute a page from an old telephone directory to each group. Groups can use a highlighter to select 25–30 telephone numbers by choosing a column in the directory and picking every tenth number.

Students can display their data by making a second line plot listing the digits zero to nine. They place an X above the digit that is the first digit of the randomly selected telephone number. They continue until all the telephone numbers have been represented from their sample.

Describing and Interpreting the Data

These questions will help students analyze their findings as they begin to formulate a solution.

➤ How does the class data compare to the data collected from the telephone book samples?

➤ How does our data help Mrs. Bell find the first digit of the telephone number? [It suggests the digits she might try first.]

➤ How can we interpret this data in a way that might help Mrs. Bell solve her problem? [Look for the column(s) with the most X's. This is the mode.]

➤ Are there any digits with no X's? Why? [Answers will vary. Telephone numbers vary from area to area; therefore, some digits may not be used in some areas.]

These are statistical terms that can be used to describe the distribution or shape of the data on a line plot.

Clusters and **gaps** Clusters are groups of points close together and possibly separated from other clusters by gaps.

Outliers An outlier is an isolated point that lies some distance away from the remainder of the data.

Mode A mode represents the data value(s) occurring most often in the data set.

Symmetry A distribution is symmetric if one half of the distribution looks like the mirror image of the other half.

Skewness A distribution is skewed if it has a long, thin tail stretching out in one direction. The direction of the skewness is the direction in which the tail is pointing.

Drawing Conclusions

These questions can help students describe their solution.

➤ Where should we collect the phone numbers to build a line plot that would be helpful to Mrs. Bell? [We should collect them in Alexander's neighborhood.]

➤ What is the advantage of a line plot? [It is a quick, easy, graphical interpretation of a small amount of data.]

Have students write a note to Mrs. Bell giving advice as to which numbers she should try if she only has three quarters to make telephone calls. Remind students to give reasons for their choices.

Additional Investigations and Projects

➤ Investigate what would happen to your class line plot if you collected data on the last digit of phone numbers.

➤ Select a short paragraph from a book and determine the letters of the alphabet that appear most frequently.

➤ Read the problem described in Ready Reference 2 (page 121). Analyze the procedure for constructing a line plot. Describe the shape of the data with some of the statistical terms learned in this investigation.

➤ Construct a line plot to examine the number of: televisions in a household, hours doing homework, exercising, or sleeping, and so on.

Counting on You

INVESTIGATION OVERVIEW

Statistical Ideas

- Constructing and interpreting **line plots**
- Finding the **mean, median,** and **mode**
- Describing shapes of data displays: **symmetry, skewness, clusters, gaps, outliers,** and **range**

Materials/Resources

Per Group:

- One sheet of clear overhead transparency
- One transparency pen
- Scissors
- Blackline Master 3, **Can We Count on You?**, page 26 (one survey for each student)
- Ready Reference 2, **Line Plots**, page 121

Understanding the Problem

Display the student transparency. Allow students to read and react to the problem. Distribute the worksheets face down.

Use these questions to facilitate discussion. They will help students organize their thoughts as they analyze the problem. You may also use questions from Ready Reference 1, page 120.

➤ How can the class data be tallied?

➤ Can the data collected from the class survey be displayed in a line plot?

➤ What kinds of things could we count about ourselves?

Can We Count on You?

How many buttons are on your clothing?

How many different colors are you wearing?

Have you ever thought about all the things you could count about yourself? Complete the survey and compare your data with the class.

TEACHING THE INVESTIGATION

Gathering and Organizing the Data

Each student should complete the survey, Can We Count on You? Divide the class into 6 groups. Assign each group one survey question. Ask students to cut the survey into 6 strips. Give each group the strips pertaining to its assigned survey question.

Have students display their data by constructing a **line plot** on a transparency.

For Primary Students:

Students may display their data in simple line plots. Have them determine the mode of their data and describe the shape of the data. Consider reading aloud the steps for constructing a line plot from Ready Reference 2 (page 121).

For Intermediate Students:

Students should construct line plots to represent the data. Students can determine the median, mode, and mean of the data. Encourage students to describe the shape of their display. Students might describe their data in terms of **clusters** and **gaps** or in terms of **symmetry** versus **skewness**.

The **mean** is the arithmetic average of a set of measurements. (You might allow students to use calculators to compute the mean.)

The **median** is the measurement that lies in the middle after the measurements are put in order from least to greatest. If there are two measurements in the middle, the median is the midpoint between the two.

The **mode** is the value that occurs most often in a data set.

Refer to Ready Reference 2 (page 121) for the steps in constructing a line plot.

Describing and Interpreting the Data

Groups can share their data displays by using the overhead projector. Advantages and disadvantages of using a line plot for each type of data should be discussed. (Answers will vary but certainly the amount of data will affect the significance of the size, shape, and interpretation.)

➤ Examine the shape of the data. Discuss **clusters, gaps,** and **outliers** depending on what the class discovered.

➤ Discuss the measures of central tendency, **median** and **mode**. Which of these measures is more representative of the data students collected?

➤ Discuss **median** and **mean**. Which of these measures is more representative of the data the students collected? Which measure indicates the most typical responses of most students? [Answer depends on data set.]

➤ Discuss the measure of the spread or variability in a set of data. Are all points close to the center (mean or median) or are the data points spread out to either side of the center?

One measure of spread is the **range** of the data. The range of a set of data is the difference between the greatest and least values. An extreme value at either end of the scale can greatly affect the range and may affect the mean.

Drawing Conclusions

Ask: How does your personal data compare with the class data?

Students may write a summary statement about the sets of data. They should be sure to include the ideas of range, symmetry, gaps, clusters, and outliers. Depending on the background of your students, they might also describe the data in terms of the median, mode, or mean.

Additional Investigations and Projects

➤ Generate a list of other items that the students in the class can count about themselves. (for example: age, height, number of family members, distance from school)

➤ Discuss the advantage of using line plots to represent counted data. Discuss the possibility of representing the data with a histogram which is a type of bar graph. (Histograms and line plots go together; they are based on measurement or counting activities. In investigations where sorting and counting are involved, a pictograph or bar graph can be used to display the data.)

Can We Count on You?
Survey

How many buttons are you are wearing on your clothing?

_____

How many different colors are you wearing?

_____

How many pieces of jewelry are you wearing?

_____

How many pieces of clothing are you wearing?

_____

How many books are in your desk?

_____

How many pencils, crayons, pens, and markers are in your desk?

_____

EQL INVESTIGATION 5

It's All in a Name

INVESTIGATION OVERVIEW

Statistical Ideas

- Surveying a group
- Making a **frequency table**
- Identifying the **median, mode,** and **mean**
- Establishing a scale

Materials/Resources

- Self-stick notes about 3" × 3" (one for each letter in each student's first name plus an additional one for each student)
- Ready Reference 2, **Line Plots**, page 121

Understanding the Problem

Display the transparency. Use these questions to facilitate discussion. They will help students organize their thoughts as they analyze the problem.

➤ How many letters are in your name?

➤ Do you think people should be able to use nicknames? Do you think using nicknames will make people's names longer or shorter?

➤ How many letters are in the shortest name? the longest name?

➤ What is the typical number of letters in a name for your class?

➤ What is the range for length of names of people in your class?

➤ Do you think this sample of people's names seems to be representative of a larger population?

➤ Do you think there are many people who will receive their first name free on the T-shirt?

How Many Letters Are in Your First Name?

Some people like T-shirts with their first names ironed on them. The first three letters of a name are free; after that, there is a 25-cent charge for each additional letter.

Will you be able to have your first name placed free?

What numbers of letters are in the first names of most of your classmates?

How much will the typical person in your class have to pay to have his or her name ironed on the T-shirt?

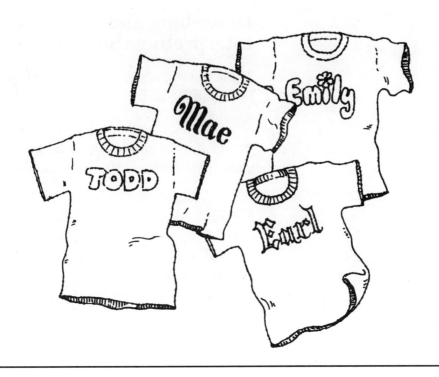

TEACHING THE INVESTIGATION

Gathering and Organizing the Data

Distribute the self-stick notes. Have students write their first name, one letter per note, and record the total number of letters in their first name on the extra note.

Members of the group will post their names in rank order from fewest letters to most letters. (See the first example below.)

Once the names are posted, the numbers can be removed from the first display and used to create a **frequency table**. (See the second example.)

Discuss the differences in the data displays. (The first method is very time consuming, but it is very visual. The second method is more abstract, and it summarizes the first picture very quickly.)

Number of Letters in Our Names

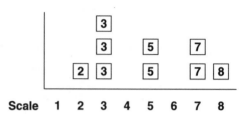

Scale 1 2 3 4 5 6 7 8

For Primary Students:

Follow the procedure above to gather and organize data but use only the mode for describing the data set.

For Intermediate Students:

Use mode and median for describing the data set. Judge the readiness of the group for a discussion of the mean.

Describing and Interpreting the Data

These questions will help students analyze their findings as they begin to formulate a solution.

➤ What is the **mode** (the most frequently occurring number)? [In this example, 3 letters.]

➤ What is the **median** length of the first names? [In this example, 5 letters. We can find this easily, since the names are ranked in numerical order and there is an odd number of responses. The center value is 5 letters.]

Letters in Our Names

2	E D
3	K I M
3	A N N
3	M A Y
5	M A R I A
5	A R N I E
7	J E S S I C A
7	R A Y M O N D
8	Y O L A N D R A

➤ Are there gaps in the data? Why? [In this example, there are no 4- or 6-letter names. In any survey, there may not be names for some of the numbers.]

➤ Describe the overall shape of the data. [Answers will vary. There may be peaks, clusters, or gaps.]

➤ What is the **mean** length of the first names? To help students understand the mean, rearrange the letters in each name until they are the same length. By manipulating the slips of paper, you can subtract letters from long names and add them to short names. The results will often be nonsense names. [In this problem, finding the mean would not be helpful in describing the data set. This may be true for other problems. For example, if filling a school bus with students, we don't use the mean because it may result in a fraction of a person. Finding the mean is not a practical solution to solving some problems.]

"Mean" Names

E	D	K	I	M
A	N	N	M	A
Y	M	A	R	I
A	A	R	N	I
E	J	E	S	S	I
C	A	R	A	Y	M
O	N	D	Y	O	L
A	N	D	R	A

Drawing Conclusions

These questions can help students describe their solutions.

➤ How many students in your class would receive names free? How does it compare to your estimate? [Answers will vary.] What name length appears to be most typical?

➤ Can you make a prediction about a larger group based on our findings? Would you have similar results if you looked at other classrooms in your school? in your state? [Answers will vary, depending on the size and make-up of the group. Students should realize that generalizations from a limited number of people can be misleading. Such a sample is not a representative sample.]

➤ What measure will be most helpful to the company selling the T-shirts: the mean, median, or mode? [A variety of opinions should be expressed. However, mode will express the most frequently used length of a name and, therefore, the most frequent purchase of additional letters.]

➤ What must we do to establish whether or not this is a representative sample? [More people have to be tested. The sample has to be randomly determined. Cultural influences must be considered.]

Additional Investigations and Projects

Is there a most popular initial (1st letter) for first names?

For Primary Students:

Construct a line plot that has the letters of the alphabet as its categories. Have students record an X above the initial letter in their first names. You may read the steps for constructing a line plot from Ready Reference 2 (page 121).

For Intermediate Students:

Survey other classes for the first initial of names and have students compare class results.

➤ If we counted syllables in the first names, what is the most frequently occurring number of syllables?

➤ Is there an association between number of syllables and length of first names? How could you construct a graph to show this association? [Label the plots from this lesson with the number of syllables per name. Do these numbers tend to cluster together? A scatter plot is another excellent method for displaying association. Upper intermediate students can use the data they have generated from this group to construct a scatter plot. Ready Reference 10 (pages 131–133) will be useful.]

➤ Gather data for the number of letters in last names of teachers in your school. Have students compute the mean and compare that to the number of letters in their last names. If the numbers are close, have students explain whether or not this indicates that they will become teachers. [There may be a coincidence of a similar number of letters occurring, but this is not a cause and effect situation.]

If the Shoe Fits

INVESTIGATION OVERVIEW

Statistical Ideas

- Gathering, organizing, and displaying data
- Measuring length to the nearest centimeter
- Finding the **median, mode, mean,** and **range**
- Observing **clusters, gaps,** and **outliers**

Materials/Resources

- Centimeter rulers (one per pair of students)
- Scissors and tape
- Blackline Master 4, **Standard Shoe Gauge**, page 39 (one gauge per pair of students)
- Ready Reference 2, **Line Plots**, page 121

Understanding the Problem

Display the transparency. Use these questions to facilitate discussion. They will help students organize their thoughts as they analyze the problem. Before collecting data, establish some guidelines for measuring foot length and tell students that one foot may be slightly larger than the other.

➤ Which foot will you measure, right or left, and does it matter? Would you leave the shoe on or take it off?

➤ Which unit of measure will you use? [Measure to the nearest centimeter.]

➤ How can we be sure that the foot is being measured accurately? [Place the zero end of the ruler at the wall and tape it in place. The student can press his or her heel against the wall as he or she steps on the ruler.]

How Big is Your Shoe?

Feet come in all sizes.

How long is your foot? How many centimeters long is it?

How does the length of your foot compare to the foot lengths of your classmates?

What is the typical foot length for students in your class?

Gathering and Organizing the Data

For Primary Students:

Have each student trace the shape of his or her foot on construction paper, cut it out, and label it with his or her name. Have students label the foot with their name. Assist students in comparing the cutouts with a centimeter ruler. This gives them experience interpreting the measurement since some estimating is required. (Ask: Is this foot closer to 10 or 11 centimeters?) Create a class line plot displaying the data or use tally marks to make a frequency table.

For Intermediate Students:

Consider asking for volunteers to demonstrate because some students might be sensitive about the size of their feet. Show how to work in pairs. One student is measured and the other student checks and records the measurement. Then the two switch roles.

Each student will determine his or her foot length. The teacher (or student assistant) records the measurements as given by the class.

Form groups of 4. Have each group determine a way to organize the class data. (This can be done in numerous ways.) Then have students display their data using line plots, bar graphs, pictographs, or tables. Some examples are shown at the bottom of this page.

Describing and Interpreting the Data

Have students share the various displays of data with the entire class and discuss the advantages and disadvantages of each type of display. Discuss which ways display the data best. Examine the shape of the data and discuss **range, clusters, gaps,** and **outliers.**

Find the **median, mode,** and **mean** for this set of data.

- The median is the middle foot length when data are organized in ascending or descending order.
- The mode is the measurement that occurs most often.
- Add all measurements and divide by the total number of measurements to find the mean. Students may use calculators.

Lesson Extension

Students have found the length of their feet in centimeters.

Line Plot

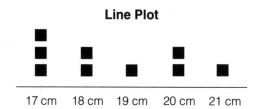

| | 17 cm | 18 cm | 19 cm | 20 cm | 21 cm |

Listing By Tally		Listing By Name		
17 cm	III	17 cm	Lynn Tyrone Judy	
18 cm	II	18 cm	Jose Kate	
19 cm	I	19 cm	Sue	
20 cm	II	20 cm	Mary Lin	
21 cm	I	21 cm	Ray	

Ask: Foot length is not the same as shoe size. How do we find our shoe size? [Allow students to discuss strategies: Some may know the size of their last pair of shoes; some may ask their parents; some may know that the size of a shoe is marked on it; some may suggest that there is a shoe gauge used by shoe salespeople.]

Ask: How do you think we can determine the typical shoe size for our class?

Give each pair of students a copy of the Standard Shoe Gauge, scissors, and tape. Have them construct the shoe gauge and then ask each student to measure the same foot again using this gauge. Have students work with their partners to be sure the heel is properly placed on the gauge. Record the measurements and create a data display of the shoe sizes. Primary students can use their foot cutouts with a gauge mounted on the chalkboard.

These questions will help students analyze their findings as they begin to formulate a solution.

➤ What is the largest size? The smallest size? Are there clusters? What is the most frequent and the least frequent shoe size? [Answers will vary according to the data collected.]

➤ Will the mean be of value in determining the typical shoe size of the group? [The mean may give a number that is not a real size, such as $6\frac{1}{4}$. Students should realize that the mode is the best indicator. The mean is

not a good measure of central tendency for size data like this.]

➤ Compare the median and mode for this set of data. Do they give similar or different information? [Sometimes the median and the mode are the same number in the data set. It depends on the spread of the data. The median and the mode are usually close and are not affected by outliers. The mean, however, can be greatly affected by outliers.]

Drawing Conclusions

These questions can help students describe their solution.

➤ Would you use mean, median, or mode to describe this data? Why? [Students should refer to the data and be able to support their answers with good reasoning.]

➤ What is the typical foot length for the class? What is the typical shoe size for the class? [Students should be able to refer to the data and make statements using statistical language.]

Additional Investigations and Projects

➤ Find out what happens when the shoe sizes of some famous athletes are added to the class data. First have students look at where the shoe sizes of these athletes fall on the standard shoe gauge. To do this, have students first work in pairs to extend the shoe gauge scale. (They can copy it, tape the copies together, and renumber the scale.) Then provide the following data: Michael Jordan, size 13 shoes; Charles Barkley, size $15\frac{1}{2}$ shoes; Patrick Ewing, size $13\frac{1}{2}$ shoes. Have students show where these sizes fall on the shoe gauge and make new representations showing the added data with the class data. Students may want to find and use shoe size data for other famous athletes as well.

When students complete the new representations, discuss these questions. How do these additions affect the interpretation of our class data? What happens to the shape of the data? [The mode won't change with the addition of these 3 pieces of data, but the median will probably be a larger shoe size. The mean will be affected most drastically, demonstrating why the mean should not be used to describe this kind of data.]

➤ Have students discuss this question, either in small groups or as a whole-class activity: If you owned a shoe store, would you stock equal amounts of each shoe size? Why or why not?

Standard Foot Gauge

Directions

1. Cut out both pieces on the solid black lines.

2. Place the bottom of the Scale piece on the dotted line at the top of the Heel piece.

3. Tape the two pieces together, being careful not to move either piece.

Scale

6
5½
5
4½
4
3½
3
2½
2
1½
1
13½
13
12½
12
11½
11
10½
10
9½
9
8½
8
7½
7
6½
6
5½
5
4½
4
3½
3
2½
2

1

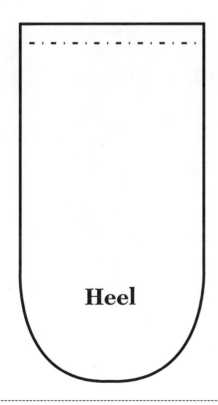

Heel

Rewind 'M Videos

INVESTIGATION OVERVIEW

Statistical Ideas

- Interpreting pictographs as **frequency tables**
- Interpreting fractions in a pictograph
- Constructing a **pictograph**

Materials/Resources

- Blackline Master 5, **Rewind 'M Video Store Rentals**, page 44 (one for each student and one overhead transparency)
- Ready Reference 3, **Pictographs and Glyphs**, page 122

Understanding the Problem

Display the transparency. Use these questions to facilitate discussion. They will help students organize their thoughts as they analyze the problem.

➤ What are some reasons for gathering this survey information? [to determine what the preferences are in the community served by the store; to match the preferences to information available about the number of children in households, and so on]

➤ What information from this pictograph is valid for our use? [The categories of videos are likely to be the same in each video store but this pictograph doesn't relate if children's movies and adult movies are mixed together. We can't tell without seeing the ratings.]

➤ Does a survey of one day of rental indicate an accurate trend for the store? [One day of rental is not a good indicator. Results will probably vary according to age of the selector (adult or child) and will probably vary according to the day of the week as well as the season.]

Which Videos Do Customers Prefer?

A recent survey of rentals for one day at the Rewind 'M Video Store is displayed in this pictograph. Use the graph to make statements and draw conclusions about the viewing habits of customers.

Type of Movie

Comedy	🎞🎞🎞🎞🎞🎞🎞
Science Fiction	🎞🎞🎞🎞🎞◧
Horror	🎞🎞🎞🎞◧
Adventure	🎞🎞🎞🎞
Musical	🎞🎞🎞◧
Romance	🎞🎞◧

🎞 = 10 rentals

TEACHING THE INVESTIGATION

Gathering and Organizing the Data

The worksheet shows the same data as the Rewind 'M Video transparency. Distribute the worksheets and have students refer to their copy as they discuss the organization of the data in the **pictograph.**

For Primary Students:

Change the key on the Rewind 'M Videos blackline master and transparency so that each symbol represents one tape. Delete or cover partial symbols. Assess the readiness of the class to interpret the graph if the key is changed so that each symbol represents 2 tapes. Then have the class determine the number of videos that a half-symbol would represent.

For Intermediate Students:

These discussion questions will help students understand how to read and interpret this pictograph.

➤ What is the value of each videotape symbol? [10 rented tapes]

➤ What is the value of a half-symbol? [5 rented tapes]

The interval for this graph, according to the key, is "10 rented tapes." Renting 5 tapes is represented with half a symbol, but how would we represent 13 rentals? [Since each symbol represents 10 rentals, it is only possible to represent multiples of five conveniently. To represent values that fall between the given intervals, in this case 13, you round to the nearest interval and approximate an answer—or you change the key.]

A symbol that represents more than one unit can be used to represent an exact value or multiples of that value. Units that are not multiples can be represented by displaying a fraction of the symbol. This involves some estimation in construction and interpretation of the pictograph. It is best to use pictures that are quick and easy to interpret. Dividing pictures into halves is easy; dividing into thirds, unless obvious, can be misleading. Dividing pictures into smaller parts than thirds should be discouraged. Choose another key in those cases, or consider another way of displaying the data.

Describing and Interpreting the Data

Work in groups to find the answers to the following interpretation questions:

➤ Which type of movie appears to be the most popular? [comedy]

➤ Which type of movie appears to be the least popular? [romance]

➤ How many comedy videos were rented? [70]

➤ What was the smallest number of any type rented? What category did that number represent? [25, Romance]

➤ What was the total number of videos rented during the period represented by the graph? [270]

Formulate questions in your group that go beyond simple interpretation. Can you detect possible flaws in creating this pictograph? [Answers will vary, but could include the following issues: not all categories are represented; some videos may be considered in two categories (action/adventure and science fiction) but are organized according to the interpretation of the store manager; an exact count can't be represented using this key; large numbers will take up too much space using this scale.]

Drawing Conclusions

These questions will help students describe their solution.

➤ Using the information in the pictograph, what recommendations would you make about future movies to be purchased for rental by the Rewind 'M Video Store? [Answers will vary but could include the following: new purchases should include titles in the most popular categories; it should be noted that this may be a temporary trend based on seasonal choices, or other Hollywood influences; continued surveying should be advised.]

➤ Discuss your conclusions with your group and present the results of your discussions to the class. Invite comments and questions.

➤ Was the method of collecting and interpreting the data adequate for drawing conclusions and projecting trends for the store? [Answers will vary. It is necessary to recognize the limitations of the information available in the pictograph. A key point of discussion should be that this was a survey taken on one day of video rental.]

➤ If the management projects that this trend is a consistent one, how will this information impact the purchasing, running, and physical setup of the store? [It may influence which aisles are chosen for particular products, how long or wide the aisles are, which posters become storefront advertisements, how many copies of each video to buy, and so on.]

Additional Investigations and Projects

➤ Make up some data and prepare a pictograph that displays results from Rewind 'M Videos during a holiday season. Refer to Ready Reference 3.

➤ Collect pictographs from public and professional publications. Include newspapers to keep data current. Display these pictographs and discuss them. Do they have flaws? Are they easy to interpret?

➤ Communicate with businesses to see how decisions are based on the gathering of statistical information.

Rewind 'M Video Store Rentals

What types of videos are most popular?

Type of Movie

Comedy

Science Fiction

Horror

Adventure

Musical

Romance

 = 10 rentals

Yakety Yak

INVESTIGATION OVERVIEW

Statistical Ideas

- Displaying multivariate data on a **facial glyph**
- Interpreting statistical information from a facial glyph

Materials/Resources

Per Student:

- Markers, crayons, eight small paper plates
- Blackline Master 6, **Yakety Yak Survey**, page 50; Blackline Master 7, **Glyph Key**, page 51
- Ready Reference 3, **Pictographs and Glyphs**, page 122

Understanding the Problem

Display the transparency. Use these questions to facilitate discussion. They will help students organize their thoughts as they analyze the problem.

➤ How many categories are we going to measure? [3]

➤ If we collect data from individuals for each category and then accumulate totals for the group, what will the category totals tell us? [High totals would be the most popular leisure time activities for the group surveyed.]

➤ What is the best way to collect and display data concerning the amount of time people in different age groups spend watching television, listening to music, and talking on the telephone? [A glyph can display the results of several categories simultaneously. Since a key is provided, each glyph can be compared to others like it. When surveying people, you can see that people who watch more television will probably listen to less music, and so on. One category will be greater than another and you can observe how several sets of data vary.]

Are Teenagers Always on the Telephone?

Some people say that teenagers are always on the telephone, listening to loud rock music, or watching television.

Do teenagers really spend more time than other people listening to music, watching television, or talking on the telephone?

Do they actually spend their time differently than people in other age groups?

Gathering and Organizing the Data

For Primary Students:

Select the main activities used in the classroom for a particular day, such as: reading books, playing with friends at recess, and listening to music. Use the glyph key and change the labels to match these activities. Create a class facial glyph for the day's activities. Select the same activities for a different day. Create a second glyph of class activities and compare it to the previous one.

For Intermediate Students:

Have students answer the three questions on the Yakety Yak survey concerning the amount of time that they spend watching television, talking on the telephone, and listening to music.

A **glyph**, derived from **hieroglyphic**, is a picture that graphically represents data that include several variables. Copy the glyph below on the chalkboard or on a blank overhead transparency.

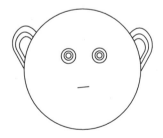

Give each student a copy of the Glyph Key. Ask students to use the key as they interpret the glyph to tell how long this person spends each day on the three activities. [Each day this person talks on the telephone for 15 minutes or less, listens to music for an hour to an hour and a half, and watches TV for 2 to 3 hours.] Symbols from the key are reproduced in the table below.

Activity	Time Spent	Symbol
Watching TV	60 min or less	eyes ○ ○
	61–120 min	◎ ◎
	121–180 min	◉ ◉
	181 min or more	◉ ◉
Listening to music	30 min or less	ears ( )
	31–60 min	(( ))
	61–90 min	((( )))
	91 min or more	(((( ))))
Talking on telephone	15 min or less	mouth ———
	16–30 min	_
	31–45 min	_/
	46 min or more	⏢

Give each student a paper plate to make a glyph of his or her personal responses to the three survey questions. Review the steps for constructing a glyph as outlined in Ready Reference 3 (page 122).

Have students survey one person from each age group listed on the Yakety Yak survey and record the data on the chart provided. They will each use 7 paper plates to make a glyph for each person they survey. Remind them to note the age group on the back of the glyph.

Describing and Interpreting the Data

Have students use facial glyphs from the various age groups to describe the habits of the people interviewed. They should then share the information that they collected with the class. During class discussion, emphasize that using the data from one person to draw conclusions about an entire age group may not be valid.

Divide the class into groups and assign each group an age category. The class should sort all the glyphs into age categories. Students use the glyphs in each age category to determine any patterns and make generalizations concerning the time spent watching television, talking on the telephone, and listening to music. Students may compile and tally the data from each glyph and determine what the typical habits of a person in that age group may be. Students will then construct one glyph representing the data for the entire age group surveyed.

Glyphs should then be shared with the entire class. Students will compare and contrast the information noted on the glyphs. Students should consider the following questions in their comparisons.

➤ Do teenagers generally spend more time on the telephone than other age groups?

➤ Do teenagers watch more television than other age groups?

➤ Do teenagers listen to music more than other age groups?

Drawing Conclusions

Have students write a paragraph comparing the data displayed on the class glyphs. These questions will help students describe their solutions.

➤ Does the data support the idea that teenagers spend more time on the telephone than people in other age groups?

➤ Do they watch television or listen to music more than other age groups?

➤ Would your conclusions have an impact on an agency that was going to market a new type of telephone?

➤ What age group would they want to target in selling a new line of telephone merchandise?

Additional Investigations and Projects

➤ Students may prepare a survey and design a glyph on a topic pertaining to favorite subjects in school, time spent on homework, or family information such as number of people in a family, number of pets, vacations, and so on.

➤ Students may construct glyphs pertaining to product information such as the fat content, sugar content, and sodium content in different brands of cereal. You may want to copy the steps for constructing a glyph from Ready Reference 3 (page 122) for students to use.

Yakety Yak Survey

Take a survey of one person in each age group to find the answers to the following questions:

➤ How many minutes a day do you talk on the telephone?

➤ How many minutes a day do you watch television?

➤ How many minutes a day do you listen to music?

Record the data you collect on the chart below.

Age	Telephone	Television	Music
1–12			
13–19			
20–29			
30–39			
40–49			
50–59			
Over 59			

Glyph Key

Watching TV

Time spent (minutes)	60 or less	61–120	121–180	181 or more
Symbol (eyes)	○ ○	◎ ◎	◉ ◉	◎ ◎

Listening to music

Time spent (minutes)	30 or less	31–60	61–90	91 or more
Symbol (ears)	( )	(( ))	((( )))	(((( ))))

Talking on telephone

Time spent (minutes)	15 or less	16–30	31–45	46 or more
Symbol (mouth)	⎯	∖_	∖_/	⟋‾⟍

Getting Keyed Up

INVESTIGATION OVERVIEW

Statistical Ideas

- Identifying attributes
- Making **frequency tables**
- Conducting a survey
- Finding **range, mean, median, mode,** and **extremes**
- Constructing a **bar graph** or **pictograph**

Materials/Resources

- Key ring with keys
- Calculators (optional)
- Blackline Master 8, **A Key Survey**, page 56
  (one for each student and a transparency of it)
- Centimeter graph paper (for each student)
- Ready Reference 4, **Bar Graphs**, page 123

Understanding the Problem

Display the transparency. Use these questions to facilitate discussion. They will help students organize their thoughts as they analyze the problem.

➤ What are the different types of keys people carry? [keys for a car or other vehicle, garage, gym locker, basement storeroom, workplace or office, and so on]

➤ How many keys do you think the typical adult carries on a key ring?

Students may realize that the occupation of the adult may determine the number of keys he or she carries. Following the discussion, students may revise their estimates.

How Many Keys Fit on a Key Ring?

The Keyhole Company manufactures key rings. Because of complaints from customers about broken rings and lost keys, they have decided to make a study of the number of keys people generally carry.

Conduct a survey to determine the typical number of keys adults carry.

TEACHING THE INVESTIGATION

Gathering and Organizing the Data

The survey will be conducted outside the classroom. Students may ask adults they know in person or by phone. This survey may be assigned as a several-day project.

Have students survey 10 or more adults about the number of keys on their key rings. They should record their data on a copy of A Key Survey, bring their results back to class, and compile a class set of data. Use a transparency of A Key Survey to record the class data. See the sample below.

Number of Keys	Adults Surveyed	Total
5							5
6			1
7					3
8									7
9				2
10			1

Have students examine the class data to find the **range**.

Describe the survey results using statistical terms, such as **median** and **mode**.

Using the frequency table, have students identify the number of people who carry fewer than 8 keys, more than 8 keys, and so on. Find the **median**. Make mathematical statements such as: "Half of the people

surveyed carry __ keys or more. Half of the people carry __ keys or fewer."

"The **mode** is _____ ."

Have the students use centimeter graph paper to construct a bar graph to display the class data.

Describing and Interpreting the Data

Have students prepare a descriptive statement about the class findings. Identify the portion of people who carry fewer than 8 keys, more than 8 keys, and so on.

These questions will help students analyze their findings as they begin to formulate a solution.

➤ Return to the smallest and largest number of keys to define the values for the **extremes**. Would these values be an important consideration for the Keyhole Company? [Making a key ring to hold the largest number of keys will not inconvenience most of the population. However, a key ring that is too small will be extremely unpopular.]

➤ Which measure (mode, median, mean, **upper extreme**) should the Keyhole Company use to show the best representation of the number of keys on a key ring?

➤ Is the adult group you surveyed representative of the adult population? Elicit occupations that might not be a representative sample [custodians, apartment managers].

Drawing Conclusions

These questions can help students describe their solutions. Students should work in groups to discuss their recommendations.

➣ Using the data, what recommendations would you make to the Keyhole Company regarding the design of the key ring?

➣ How many keys would you recommend the key ring hold?

➣ Are you basing your recommended number on the mode, mean, or upper extreme?

➣ Do we need more information than just the number of keys to make a good recommendation to the Keyhole Company for improving their design? [the kind of clasp, the materials of construction, the design, and so on]

➣ Are there other variables that would contribute to broken key rings besides the number of keys? [key size, key shape, and so on]

➣ How would the type of keys affect the data? [Keys for late-model cars tend to be longer than those for older cars. Sizes of keys vary. Original keys are heavier than duplicate key copies. Length and weight of keys can cause key rings to wear out and break.]

Additional Investigations and Projects

Conduct a survey in which you tally types of keys carried by adults.

For Primary Students:

Construct a pictograph, line plot, or bar graph to display data for the type of keys carried by the adults. Place the data displays on a bulletin board. Identify the mode to show the number of house, vehicle, office, mail box, and miscellaneous keys. Review steps for constructing a pictograph from Ready Reference 3 (p. 122).

For Intermediate Students:

Use calculators to estimate the percentage of each type of key carried by the surveyed adults. Report to the class on your findings. Compare the results. Combine data from all groups to make a chart and use calculators to estimate the percentage of each type for the combined class survey data.

A Key Survey

Survey 10 or more adults to find the numbers of keys adults generally carry on a key ring. Tally the findings using the frequency table below. Then write a paragraph about the data.

Number of Keys	Adults Surveyed	Total
2		
3		
4		
5		
6		
7		
8		
9		
10		

My Survey Results:

_____

_____

_____

_____

EQL INVESTIGATION 10

Peanuts by the Handful

INVESTIGATION OVERVIEW

Statistical Ideas

- Surveying a group
- Making a **frequency table** and a **bar graph**
- Establishing an appropriate **scale**
- Making comparisons and looking for **associations**

Materials/Resources

One Per Group:

- Bowl of peanuts (shell on) or counters
- Blackline Master 9, **Peanuts by the Handful Data Table**, page 63
- Blackline Masters 10, 11, 12, and 13, **Peanuts by the Handful, Grids A, B, C, and D**, pages 64–67
- Ready Reference 4, **Bar Graphs**, page 123

Understanding the Problem

Display the transparency. Use these questions to facilitate discussion. They can help students organize their thoughts as they analyze the problem.

➤ What are the factors that will influence the number of peanuts that can be held by the person? [Size is a factor: size of hand, size of peanuts, and so on.]

➤ Are there differences between a regular handful and a competitive handful? [A competitive handful usually holds more peanuts, the hold is not natural.]

➤ Will there be a significant difference in the number of peanuts the students can pick up? [Results will vary.]

How Many Peanuts Can You Hold?

It is snack time. On the table, there is a bowl of peanuts with their shells on. All students are invited to take a handful of peanuts from the bowl. Will each student take about the same amount?

Estimate the range for a sample handful of peanuts for the members of your group.

Gathering and Organizing the Data

Have students work in groups of 3 or 4. Before taking a sample handful (or observing others), have students estimate how many peanuts they can hold in one hand. Then have 20 students take a sample handful, count and record the number, and return the sample to the bowl. Each group should record results on the Peanuts By The Handful Data Table (see sample below).

Participant	Number of Peanuts
A	4
B	6
C	7
D	5
E	5
F	4
G	7
H	6

Give each group one set of Grids A–D. Each group will prepare a **bar graph** of the compiled data using each of the grids. Expect discussion and verification by students within each group. When constructing the graphs, groups should rank the data (that is, order the data from greatest to least on their grids) so that comparisons are easier to make. Each group should review and discuss which grid (A, B, C, or D) is the most effective in displaying and analyzing the data. Why?

[Through discussion within the groups, students should discover the differences in scaling for each of the prepared grids. The **scale** used on a graph can determine how easy or difficult it is to construct and interpret. Visual displays should be easy to read. Graph A, scaled by 1s, may not provide enough room to record all samples. Graph C, scaled by 5s, is too difficult to interpret, and so on.] See annotated grids below. Note that these show just part of the entire grid.

Grids A, B, and C have scales that vary on the *y*-axis. This example is scaled by 2s. The other graphs are scaled by 1s and 5s. Each produces a vertical bar graph of different heights for the same data.

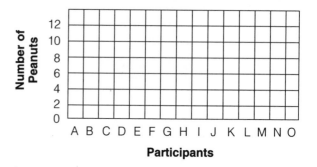

Grid D switches the *x* and *y* axes. It produces a horizontal bar graph of the same data.

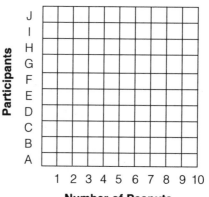

For Primary Students:

Make a series of graphs as you lead a discussion to help students discover choices in graphing. Judge the readiness of the group for scaling by 2s and 5s.

For Intermediate Students:

Allow students to make a series of graphs to discover the differences and difficulties encountered with the change of the scale. For those students who are more experienced, supply different-sized graph paper (centimeter and quarter-inch) to further demonstrate differences and difficulties encountered with the change of scale.

Describing and Interpreting the Data

Have a student from each group present Grid A. Compare all the graphs and discuss what problems may have been encountered with Grid A. Do the same for Grids B, C, and D.

Use these questions to help students analyze their findings as they begin to formulate a solution.

➤ After discussing the various graphs, discuss the attributes of the graphs. What are some problems with the displays? [Scale is so spread out that the important focus of the center of the data is pushed to the perimeter of the page, scale is so cluttered that differences are difficult to distinguish, and so on.]

➤ What makes an effective graph? [Display of data is centered on the page—not pushed to the top or crowded to one side, differences can be easily seen, and so on.]

➤ What contributes to the ease of reading? [a scale that accurately and effectively shows the data]

➤ What information did you learn from this group about handful size? (Use the statistical terms: range, mode, gaps, outliers, and so on, in your discussion.) For example, are there any data points that lie well outside the general spread of the data? If so, you may have an outlier. Did your group have one outlier? More than one outlier?

You might gather the earlier class estimates of the number of peanuts the group thought constituted a handful, and compare them to the mode.

➤ Do the results vary depending on the size of the hand? [Generally, the larger the hand, the more peanuts the person can grab. However, there can be exceptions.]

➤ Can the data be interpreted using the mean? [Yes, in attempting to estimate the number of peanuts to serve to the class for a party or celebration, it would be helpful to know the average serving per person.]

➤ Is there a way that we can make the servings more uniform? [Yes, supply a scoop. This creates a new question: How many peanuts constitute an average scoopful?]

Drawing Conclusions

These questions can help students describe their solutions.

➤ Why is it important to consider range before beginning construction of the graph? [It is important to review and consider the range of the data before selecting the scale, then space off or visualize how the data will spread before beginning the construction of the graph, or there might not be enough space on the paper. For intermediate students, the coordinate grid might not be provided by the teacher. Selection of the proper size graph paper is another important factor to consider.]

➤ Why is scale important to the interpretation of the data? [It is important to select a scale that will facilitate ease of reading and correctness of interpretation.]

➤ Were estimates close to the actual amounts picked? [Answers will vary.]

➤ What was the typical handful for your group? [Answers will vary. Students should justify responses by using the mode, median, or mean.]

➤ Will this information help other teachers to determine how many peanuts to buy for snack time for other classes? [It may give a rough estimate; however, the sample size is too small. There are many other factors to consider that affect group size and number of peanuts consumed: Are other foods being served? Do all students like peanuts? Do older students eat more? How long ago did students have a meal? Are they hungry?]

Additional Investigations and Projects

For Primary Students:

Supply one bowl of peanuts per group and a large spoon or scoop. Each member of the group will scoop out a serving of peanuts. Make a class graph of the results.

For Intermediate Students:

➤ Supply one bowl of centimeter cubes per group of four. Instruct each team to make a group estimate of the total number of centimeter cubes that can be grabbed by the whole group. Construct a double bar graph of the estimated amount and the actual amount for each team.

➤ Use the data from the Peanuts by the Handful sampling lesson. Record the data for each participant on individual index cards and place them in a shoe box. Shake. Select 12 pieces of data at random from the data cards in the shoe box. Graph the data. Return those 12 index cards. Shake and repeat the process of selecting and graphing 12 more pieces of data. Compare the graphs. Are the results the same as the first sample of 12? What results would you expect if you selected and graphed 12 more data cards?

Peanuts by the Handful Data Table

Participant	Number of Peanuts
A	
B	
C	
D	
E	
F	
G	
H	
I	
J	
K	
L	
M	
N	
O	
P	
Q	
R	
S	
T	

Peanuts by
the Handful

Grid A

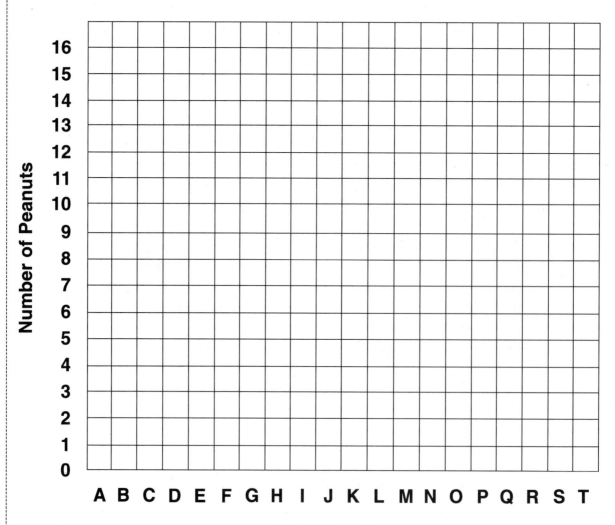

Peanuts by the Handful

Grid B

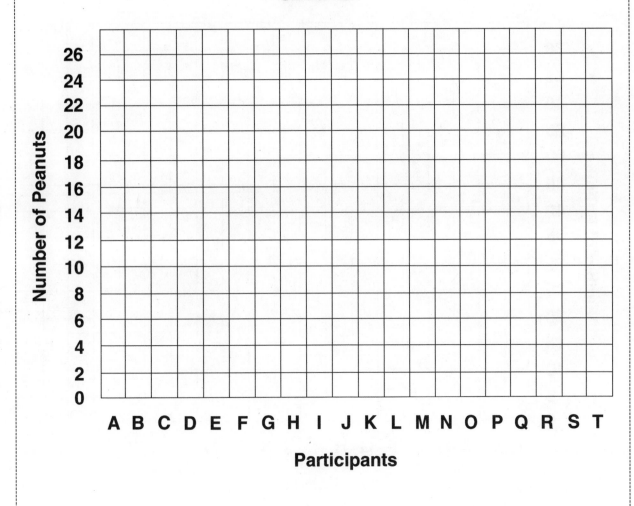

Peanuts by the Hanful

Grid C

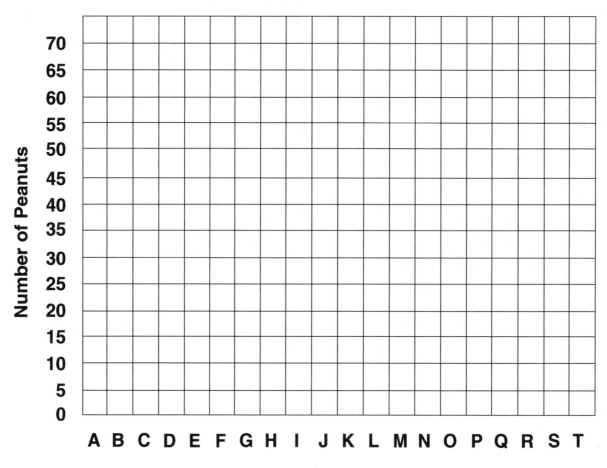

Peanuts by the Handful

Grid D

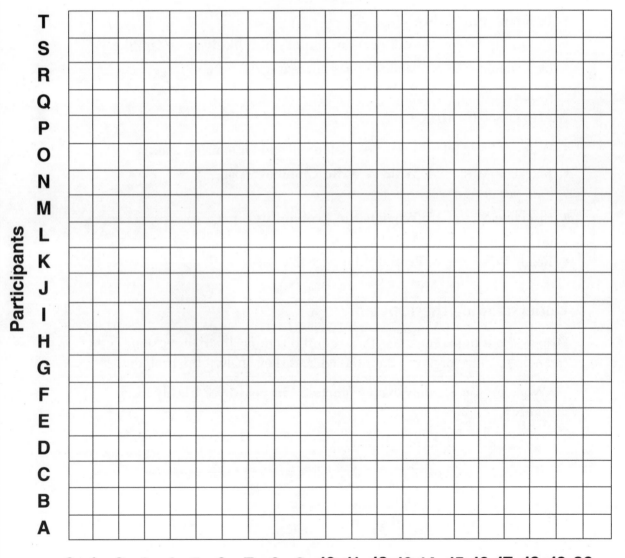

Number of Peanuts

What Are the Chances?

INVESTIGATION OVERVIEW

Statistical Ideas

- Defining **probability**
- Exploring the concepts of **certain, impossible, likely** versus **unlikely**
- Determining the probability of a given **event**

Materials/Resources

- Walk-on Probability Scale (See Gathering and Organizing Data)
- Blackline Master 14, **What Are the Chances?**, page 72 (one per group)
- Blackline Master 15, **What Is the Probability?**, page 73 (one overhead transparency)
- Ready Reference 5, **Probability**, page 124

Understanding the Problem

Display the transparency. Use these questions to facilitate discussion. They can help students organize their thoughts as they analyze the problem.

➤ What are some events that are **certain? impossible? highly likely? unlikely?**

➤ How would you define probability?

➤ How does the idea of probability relate to real life situations?

What Are the Chances?

Is it certain, highly likely, unlikely, or impossible?

➤ You will have homework tonight.

➤ It will rain today.

➤ You will ride in a truck this week.

➤ The next baby born in your town will be a girl.

➤ You will be in school tomorrow.

➤ A coin will land "heads" every time it is tossed.

TEACHING THE INVESTIGATION

Gathering and Organizing the Data

Ask students to name more events in their lives that are certain, impossible, likely, and unlikely to happen.

Divide the class into groups. Give each group a copy of What Are the Chances?, page 69, and discuss the probability of the occurrence of each **event**. Students will then assign the events to a place on a probability scale from 0 through 1.

Zero represents the probability that an event will not occur, and 1 represents the probability that an event is certain to occur.

Use a long piece of tape or ribbon to make a walk-on probability scale. Make sure that the scale is clearly marked with a 0, $\frac{1}{2}$, and 1. Ask students to share their ideas by having one person from each group stand on the probability line in the place that represents their group's ideas about the chances of a particular event occurring.

Walk-On Probability Scale

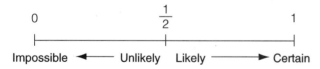

Describing and Interpreting the Data

Generate a list of words associated with various values of probability: *likely, unlikely, probable,* and so on.

For Intermediate Students:

Discuss ways to express probability such as: percents, fractions, and ratios. The ways to express a probability would reflect the experience, age, and ability level of the class. (1 out of 4, $\frac{1}{4}$, 0.25, 25%)

Display a transparency of What Is the Probability? Have each student rank the events from the least likely to occur to most likely to occur. Ask individual students to present and justify their responses. You might make 5 cards with the letters A, B, C, D, and E for students to place on the Walk-On Probability Scale.

[Answers will vary; therefore, have students discuss the reasons for selecting a specific order. For example, a student whose family owns a red car may list that as *E*, a most likely event. Point out that it is true for that student but perhaps not as likely for other students.]

Walk-On Probability Scale

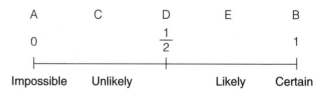

Drawing Conclusions

These questions can help students describe their solutions.

➤ What does it mean for an event to have a probability of 1? [The event is certain to occur.]

➤ What does it mean for an event to have a probability of 0? [The event will not occur.]

➤ What does it mean for an event to have a probability of 0.2 or $\frac{2}{10}$? [There is a small chance that the event will occur.]

➤ Why does the value of 1 refer to an event that is certain to occur? [Refer to the definition of probability as the number of favorable outcomes divided by the number of possible outcomes. For example, 5 out of 5 is $\frac{5}{5}$ or 1]

Have students list three events representing three different probability values that could occur in their lives. Discuss and analyze the events and probabilities students listed.

Additional Investigations and Projects

➤ Have students use a graphic organizer such as a web to classify events that are impossible, certain, likely, and unlikely to happen.

➤ Play the Outcomes Game. It may be used to assess students' understanding of probability. Make a transparency of Blackline Master 16, How to Play the Outcomes Game, page 74. Give each student a copy of Blackline Master 17, Outcomes Game Board, page 75, and a marker.

Teacher Note for Outcomes Game:

After reading and explaining the rules, play Round 1 of the game. Create a chart on the chalkboard and tally the results. (Be sure to place a tally mark next to every answer that is true about each drawing. There may be several answers that are true.) After each selection of 3 cubes ask: "Who moved a space this time?" Ask students to justify their moves. Reinforce their understanding of the terms *at least, all,* and *no.*

At the conclusion of the game ask:

➤ What choices were good ones? Why?

➤ If you were to play again, would you change your choice? Why?

Play the second round. Point out that a different Outcome may be chosen for this round. For each draw have students raise hands to explain when they advance one space. Discuss final results. Before playing the third round, consider asking students to make the following changes to statements 7 and 8. Cross off "at least" and put "only" in its place.

Discuss how this will change the results.

What Are the Chances?

Think about each of the following events. Discuss with your group how likely each is to occur. Decide where each event would be located on this scale. Place the letter for each event below on the appropriate place on the scale.

What are the chances for each event?

A. You will have homework tonight.

B. The next baby born in your town will be a girl.

C. It will rain in your town today.

D. You will watch television some time today.

E. You will be struck by lightning.

F. You will eat or drink something red today.

G. You will eat something in the next four hours.

H. You will read at least four books this month.

I. You will ride in a truck this week.

J. You will get the flu this year.

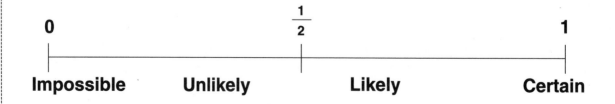

What is the Probability?

Consider each of the following events and the probability that it may occur.

Put the events in order from the least likely to occur to the most likely to occur by deciding where you would place the letter for each event on the Probability Scale.

What are the chances?

A. You will win a million dollars.

B. You will see a red car today.

C. You will get the flu this year.

D. A coin you flip will land on heads.

E. It will snow this year in Colorado.

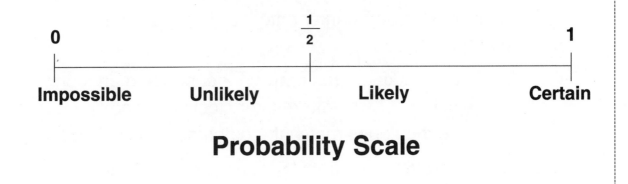

Probability Scale

How to Play the Outcomes Game

Materials:

■ A copy of the Outcomes Game Board and a marker for each player

■ 1 bag containing 5 yellow cubes, 4 red cubes, and 1 green cube

Rules:

1. Everyone places a marker on START.

2. Keep in mind that 3 cubes at a time will be drawn from the bag and then returned to the bag.

3. Decide which Outcome is most likely and put a check mark next to it in the column for that round.

4. One player draws 3 cubes from the bag and announces the colors of the cubes to the group.

5. If the Outcome you checked is true for the 3 chosen cubes, move your marker onto the game board to the letter "O."

6. Continue by taking turns drawing 3 cubes and announcing the colors. Move your marker clockwise one space each time the cubes match the outcome you checked.

7. The first player to land on "S" wins the game and shouts, "Outcomes!"

Outcomes
Game Board

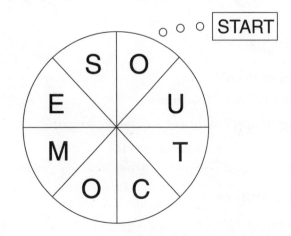

Outcomes	Round 1	Round 2	Round 3
There is a green cube.			
All the cubes are yellow.			
All the cubes are the same color.			
There are no green cubes.			
There is one cube of each color.			
There are two yellow cubes.			
At least one cube is yellow.			
At least one cube is red.			
All of the cubes are red.			

The World at Your Fingertips

INVESTIGATION OVERVIEW

Statistical Ideas

- **Simulating** an event
- Determining **relative frequency**
- **Estimating** the probability of an event occurring
- Exploring **mutually exclusive events**

Materials/Resources

- Inflatable globe
- Blackline Master 18, **The Earth's Surface**, page 80
  (one overhead transparency)
- Blackline Master 19, **World at Your Fingertips**, page 81
  (one copy for intermediate classes)
- Blackline Master 20, **Does It Hit Land or Water?**, page 82
  (one copy for primary classes)
- Ready Reference 6, **Simulation: A Probability Experiment**,
  pages 125–126

Understanding the Problem

Display the transparency. Use these questions to facilitate discussion. They
can help students organize their thoughts as they analyze the problem.

➤ Do you think the meteorite is more likely to hit the land or the water?
Explain.

➤ What previous knowledge do you have about the surface of the Earth
that will help you to make a prediction?

➤ If the meteorite hits land, is it likely to hit North America? How can we
use simulation to investigate this question?

Where Will the Meteorite Land?

A large meteorite has just been spotted in the Earth's orbit and is expected to hit the Earth's surface next week.

> ➤ What is the probability that the meteorite will hit the land surface?

> ➤ What is the probability that the meteorite will hit the water surface?

> ➤ Is it likely the meteorite will strike North America?

> ➤ Should you be worried about your family's safety?

Gathering and Organizing the Data

We can't wait for a series of meteorites to hit the Earth, but we can model the event happening. This technique of creating an experiment that will model a real world experiment is called simulation. Simulations allow us to study properties of real-world events that are too complicated, too expensive, or impossible to actually observe.

Discuss ways to simulate this event.

Conduct the following simulation as a class activity.

Place a red dot on the tip of each student's right index finger with an overhead marker. This will represent the meteorite. Students will toss an inflatable globe to each other with a spin. Each person will catch the globe with two hands. He or she will tell where the meteorite (the red dot on his or her finger) landed. Have the class make a prediction about the outcome of the experiment and record that prediction on the tally sheet. Toss the globe 100 times. Each outcome is reported to the recorder who will tally the results and will inform the class when 100 tosses are complete. (Two globes will save time.)

For Primary Students:

Students will tell whether they think the meteorite will hit land or water. Use Does It Hit Land or Water? to record their predictions and their data.

For Intermediate Students:

Older students will be able to state which continent or body of water was the landing spot. A geography review may be necessary to help students identify continents and oceans. All data should be recorded on World at Your Fingertips. Select a person to record the data and to signal the next toss. Select another person to tally the total number of tosses and to alert the group when 100 tosses are complete.

Once the students have returned to their seats, the recorder can report the total tally for each continent and ocean. Each student should record the count, then express it as a **relative frequency** (the number of times the event occurred divided by the total number of tosses) and as a percent. The actual percentages can later be displayed on the overhead for students to copy and compare.

The experimental values may not be the same as those listed on The Earth's Surface. Remind students that this is a simulation and although totals may not be exact, they should be close if we perform enough trials. Consider challenging students who are able to research the actual percentages using an atlas or almanac rather than your supplying it for the students.

Describing and Interpreting the Data

These questions can help students analyze their findings as they begin to formulate a solution.

➤ What is the probability of the meteorite hitting the water? How did you obtain your results? [≈ 70% or about 70 tosses out of 100 hit water]

➤ What is the probability of the meteorite hitting the land? How did you obtain your results? [≈ 30% or about 30 tosses out of 100 hit land]

➤ Were the results what you expected? Explain. [Answers will vary. One example may be: we expected the meteorite to hit the water more often, but we did not expect it to hit there as often as it did. We know there is about three times more water than hit so we expect the meteorite to land there about three times more often.]

Have students determine the probability of the meteorite hitting North America or one of the other six continents. Discuss the chance of this event occurring.

Display the transparency so that students can examine the data on The Earth's Surface. Then they can compare their experimental results with the predicted results.

Ask: What is the probability of the meteorite hitting the land? [29%] What is the probability of the meteorite hitting the water? [71%]

Discuss the fact that these two events cannot overlap. If a meteorite hits earth, it will either hit land or water. These events are said to be **mutually exclusive**. The sum of the probabilities of mutually exclusive favorable events is equal to 1.

P (Hitting the land) + P (Hitting the water) = 1

Another example of a mutually exclusive event is the tossing of a coin. It will land heads or tails. The sum of both probabilities equals 1.

Drawing Conclusions

Have students write a report indicating what they believe will happen when the meteorite hits the Earth. Have them include the results of the class simulation as well as the results obtained from the data given about surface area. Students should also include the similarities or differences in the results and provide an explanation for their conclusions. Could this simulation have been executed in a more accurate manner, and if so, how?

Additional Investigations and Projects

Conduct a simulation to determine the probability of the meteorite hitting the United States. Using a map or other source of information, determine the area of the United States and develop the probability of the meteorite hitting the United States. Have students design the experiment and the categories in which to record data.

The Earth's Surface

Land Surface	Approximate Area	% of Earth
North America	9,400,000 square miles	5
South America	6,900,000 square miles	3
Europe	3,800,000 square miles	2
Asia	17,400,000 square miles	9
Africa	11,700,000 square miles	6
Australia	3,300,000 square miles	1
Antarctica	5,400,000 square miles	3
Other	500,000 square miles	0
Total Land	**58,400,000 square miles**	**29**

Water Surface	Approximate Area	% of Earth
Atlantic Ocean	33,420,000 square miles	17
Pacific Ocean	64,186,000 square miles	33
Indian Ocean	28,350,000 square miles	14
Arctic Ocean	5,106,000 square miles	3
Other	8,705,000 square miles	4
Total Water	**140,000,000 square miles**	**71**

World at Your Fingertips

Place	Tally	Count	Relative Frequency	Percent
North America				
South America				
Europe				
Asia				
Africa				
Australia				
Antarctica				
Other				

Place	Tally	Count	Relative Frequency	Percent
Arctic Ocean				
Atlantic Ocean				
Indian Ocean				
Pacific Ocean				
Other				

Does It Hit
Land or Water?

	Land	Water
Predictions		
Data		

Mystery Spinners

INVESTIGATION OVERVIEW

Statistical Ideas

- Determining the **outcomes**
- Estimating the probability of an event occurring
- Making a **frequency table** and **bar graph**

Materials/Resources

- Large sheets of poster paper, markers or crayons
- Blackline Master 21, **The Big Wheel,** page 88 (one for each student)
- Ready Reference 5, **Probability,** page 124

Understanding the Problem

Display the transparency. Use these questions to facilitate discussion. They can help students organize their thoughts as they analyze the problem.

➤ What are all the possible outcomes on the spinner?

➤ How many times in total did they spin the spinner last year?

➤ Did one or more of the colors have a higher frequency than the others?

➤ Would this affect the way you would reconstruct the spinner?

➤ How does the fact that Iva Memory remembers that there were 10 equal parts help in making a new spinner?

Can You Describe the Carnival Spinner?

It is math carnival time in the fifth grade at Catonsville School, and the giant color spinner is missing! The students want to design a large spinner just like the one used last year. Unfortunately, no one can remember what the spinner looked like, except for one feature.

Iva Memory, the class historian, remembered that the spinner was divided into 10 equal parts.

Fortunately, Seymour Tally, the class treasurer, had recorded all the spins from last year's carnival. There were:

18 blue	8 purple
11 yellow	13 pink
11 red	22 green
8 black	9 white

How can the class use this data to help make a spinner like the one used last year?

TEACHING THE INVESTIGATION

Gathering and Organizing the Data

Divide students into groups. Give each student a copy of The Big Wheel. Ask students to use the data from Seymour Tally to color the regions of the spinner so that it probably looks like the spinner used at last year's carnival.

Students in each group can then share their spinners and discuss why they chose to color their spinner in a particular way. [Based on the data, 2 of the 10 regions would likely be blue and 2 would probably be green with 1 region for each of the remaining 6 colors. Students should understand that these are still guesses based on the results of spinning a spinner and nothing can actually be proven since the original spinner cannot be found.]

Give each group a mystery spinner which will not be shown to anyone in the class. Mystery spinners can be made inexpensively from poster paper by following these directions.

Making a Mystery Spinner:

Draw a circle on a piece of tag board or poster paper. Divide the circle into regions and color each region. Place a paper fastener through a paper clip and secure it to the middle of the circle. Adjust the paper fastener so that the paper clip spins freely.

Have each group conduct a probability experiment by spinning the spinner 25–30 times and recording the outcome of each spin in a frequency table. Before they begin the experiment, ask each group to predict what they think will happen in the experiment. Afterwards each group will make a chart or bar graph of the data.

Groups will then take turns sharing their data displays with the entire class while being careful not to show their mystery spinner. The rest of the class will describe the spinner based on their interpretation of the data. After these descriptions have been given, the groups will reveal their mystery spinners.

For Primary Students:

This mystery spinner lesson may be adapted for primary students by dividing all the circles into fourths and telling the students that they have been divided in that way. Provide the groups with a frequency table to record their data.

For Intermediate Students:

Students may want to design their own mystery spinners and ask other students to guess their design.

Describing and Interpreting the Data

As you describe each group's spinner consider the following ideas.

➤ Based on the data collected, what are all the possible outcomes? [all the colors on which the spinner landed]

86   **Section V: Probability**

➤ What are the chances that there was another possible outcome on which the spinner did not land? [Answers will vary but when using 25–30 spins, it is likely that all the outcomes would appear at least once. Students may decide that if the spinner lands on a line it will not be counted as an outcome. They will spin again.]

➤ What color did the spinner land on the least? [the color with the lowest number of spins]

➤ Is there one outcome that occurs more often than others? Is there a logical explanation for this? [The results could vary according to the force used to hit the spinner. Some techniques can produce a pattern of results.]

➤ If you were going to spin the spinner, on what color do you think that it would most likely land? [This should be the color with the highest frequency.]

➤ How could you improve your chances of making the correct prediction? [Increase the number of spins.]

Drawing Conclusions

Have students write a brief paragraph describing one of the group's mystery spinners. They should include all the possible outcomes as well as statistical evidence to support their statements. [Example: I think that Group A's spinner is divided into 4 equal parts, with 3 sections that are blue and 1 that is yellow. All of their spins landed on blue or yellow. I think that the blue part is bigger than the yellow part because it landed on blue more than it landed on yellow. It landed on blue 16 times and it only landed on yellow 4 times.]

Students could make a drawing of the other groups' spinners.

Additional Investigations and Projects

➤ Give students a set of desired outcomes for a spinner investigation. Have students design a spinner that would be highly likely to produce the given results. (Example: Design a spinner that in 25 spins, would land on red about 15 times, on white about 5 times, and on blue about 5 times.)

➤ Students may collect information on the odds of winning certain contests and lotteries in their state. Many contests now are required to print the odds of winning somewhere on their advertisement.

➤ Students may design a children's board game that requires a spinner. Careful thought will be needed to make a spinner that will advance play as well as offer challenges to the players. The game could be evaluated for fairness.

The Big Wheel

Seymour Tally recorded this data from last year's carnival.

Blue	‖‖‖ ‖‖‖ ‖‖‖ |||
Yellow	‖‖‖ ‖‖‖	
Red	‖‖‖ ‖‖‖	
Black	‖‖‖ |||
Purple	‖‖‖ |||
Pink	‖‖‖ ‖‖‖ |||
Green	‖‖‖ ‖‖‖ ‖‖‖ ‖‖‖ ||
White	‖‖‖ ||||

Use the data above to predict the colors on the spinner.

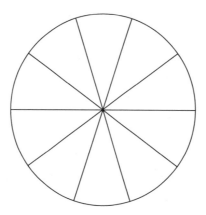

EQL INVESTIGATION 14

Nuttie Buddies

INVESTIGATION OVERVIEW

Statistical Ideas

- Making a **stem and leaf plot**
- Determining **variation**
- Establishing proportions in order to **make predictions**
- Calculating **rates** per hour, per day, per year

Materials/Resources

Per Student Pair:

- One bolt that is 2 inches long and $\frac{1}{4}$-inch in diameter, one washer, three nuts, two 6-inch pipe cleaners, and one 3-inch pipe cleaner per Nuttie Buddie
- One-centimeter graph paper (optional for primary students)
- Stop watch or clock
- Calculator (optional)
- Blackline Master 22, **Nuttie Buddie Assembly Instructions**, page 95
- Ready Reference 7, **Stem and Leaf Plots**, pages 127–128

Understanding the Problem

Display the transparency. Use these questions to facilitate discussion.

➤ How long will it take one person to construct one Nuttie Buddie?

➤ How many Nuttie Buddies can be constructed by an average person in one hour?

➤ How can you project these results across a normal 8-hour work day, a 24-hour day, and a 5-day week?

➤ Is it faster to use an assembly line to construct the Nuttie Buddies? What are the effects of working on an assembly line?

How Fast Can You Make a Nuttie Buddie?

Nuttie Buddies, Inc. is opening a new plant in your home town! The management needs to compute the number of Nuttie Buddies that can be constructed during any given period so they can project costs and fill the avalanche of orders.

Can you predict the number of Nuttie Buddies that can be produced in any given period of time?

Should the Nuttie Buddies be constructed by a single craftsperson or would an assembly line be a better choice?

TEACHING THE INVESTIGATION

Gathering and Organizing the Data

Distribute the Nuttie Buddie Assembly Instructions. Have students look closely at a Nuttie Buddie and read the assembly instructions. Allow time for them to practice the step-by-step construction of this modern miracle (just to work out the bugs...).

Have students work in teams of two. As one person constructs a Nuttie Buddie, the other records the time in seconds. Continue the process until each member of the team has completed a time trial. Students can display the data in a **stem and leaf plot.**

To make a **stem and leaf plot,** find the smallest and largest numbers. For example, if the data ranged from 30 through 150 seconds, the stems would be the numbers in the tens and hundreds columns. Write the stems vertically with a line drawn to the right.

Separate each number into a stem and a leaf. Put the leaves (the digit in the ones column) on the plot to the right of the stem. Continue until all the numbers have been placed on the plot. Then on a new plot arrange the leaves from the smallest value to the largest value.

Be sure to include a key on the stem and leaf plot. Look at this example. It represents 38 time trials ranging from 30 seconds to 154 seconds.

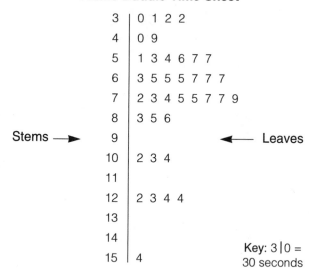

Nuttie Buddie Time Sheet

```
 3 | 0 1 2 2
 4 | 0 9
 5 | 1 3 4 6 7 7
 6 | 3 5 5 5 7 7 7
 7 | 2 3 4 5 5 7 7 9
 8 | 3 5 6
 9 |
10 | 2 3 4
11 |
12 | 2 3 4 4
13 |
14 |
15 | 4
```

Stems → 9 ← Leaves

Key: 3|0 = 30 seconds

For Primary Students:

Use graph paper to help students keep the columns ordered. If students have too much difficulty constructing a Nuttie Buddie, they could make macaroni shell necklaces. Students could also be timed on the length of time it takes to put together a simple puzzle. Students may need help in keeping time and converting minutes to seconds.

For Intermediate Students:

➤ Calculate the number of Nuttie Buddies that each person could make in one hour. [Students will need to determine the number of seconds in an hour. (60 sec × 60 min in an hour = 3600 seconds) Then they divide 3600 seconds by the time it takes to construct one Nuttie Buddie to see how many Nuttie Buddies that person could make at that rate.]

➤ Will this be an accurate prediction? Why or why not? [Answers will vary.]

Describing and Interpreting the Data

These questions can help students analyze their findings as they begin to formulate a solution.

➤ Looking at the stem and leaf plot, how can we determine the average time it takes a worker to make a Nuttie Buddie?

➤ Discuss the shape of the data. Where does it cluster? Are there gaps? Are there any outliers?

➤ Determine what a typical worker will produce in one hour. [Find the median and the mean and compare.]

➤ What causes the mean to be larger (or smaller)? [Usually skewness, depending on how extreme the values are that skew the mean.]

➤ Using that information, **predict** the number of Nuttie Buddies that can be produced in: (a) an 8-hour shift [eight times the number per hour], (b) a 24-hour day [twenty-four times the number per shift], and (c) a 5-day work week [five times the daily number]. Calculators may be used to do the calculations.

➤ What factors might cause the predictions to be inaccurate? [Answers will vary, but will most certainly include worker fatigue, union contracted breaks and lunch times, sloppy construction due to boredom, and so on.]

➤ If Nuttie Buddies, Inc. receives an emergency order for 5,000 Nuttie Buddies from Toys Are Anybody Else, how many days would it take the average person in your class, working 24 hours a day, to fill the order? [5,000 ÷ (24 × the number of Nuttie Buddies per hour) or let d = number of days and n = the number of Nuttie Buddies per hour, then $d = \frac{5000}{24n}$]

➤ How many people would it take to complete the order, based on that average, in 24 hours? [5,000 ÷ the number of days or $\frac{5000}{d}$]

➤ How does the average time it takes for one worker to make a Nuttie Buddie compare with the time it takes to make a Nuttie Buddie on an assembly line? [In some cases a single worker might be faster, but results may not be consistent. For factory assembly time, the best results will be the consistent and reliable results. Assembly line work makes results more uniform.

Drawing Conclusions

These questions can help students describe their solution.

➣ How does the stem and leaf plot enable us to view the variation in performance? [The plot helps us easily view the shape of the data. We can see the spread of the time trials. The stem and leaf plot contains all the original data points.]

➣ Why is it important to discover the variation before determining the average performance? [Average performance can be interpreted as the mean or median. Large variations in data misrepresent the mean.]

Additional Investigations and Projects

➣ Brainstorm ways to formulate an assembly line procedure to increase production. Have groups of four students form an assembly line and conduct a time trial. Students in the class can then make a stem and leaf plot displaying data on assembly line time trials. Data could also be compared with individual time trials using a back-to-back stem and leaf plot. See Ready Reference 9 (see page 130).

➣ Use stem and leaf plots to collect and interpret class data involving: number of servings of fruits and vegetables consumed in one day or the numbers of episodes of violence seen on television between 7 P.M. and 10 P.M. A stem and leaf plot can also be used to organize a collection of pennies or nickels according to their dates.

Nuttie Buddie Assembly Instructions

Nuttie Buddie Inc.
Parts List

$\frac{1}{4}$" bolt, 2" in length   washer   3 nuts

one 3" pipe cleaner, two 6" pipe cleaners

Step 1: Slide on washer.

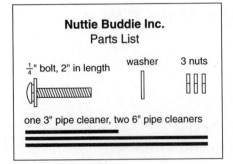

Step 2: Screw on 1st nut.

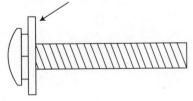

Step 3: Screw on 2nd nut.

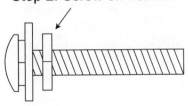

Step 4: Screw on 3rd nut.

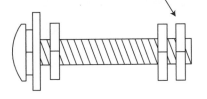

Step 5: Twist antenna between bolt head and washer.

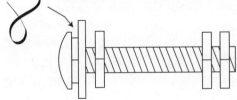

Step 6: Twist leg between washer and 1st nut.

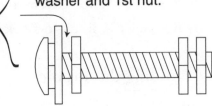

Step 7: Twist leg around bolt between 2nd nut and 3rd nut.

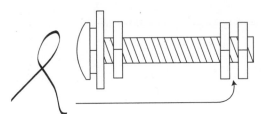

Step 8: Bend each leg at the bottom to form feet.

Trashball Hoops

INVESTIGATION OVERVIEW

Statistical Ideas

- Making a **back-to-back stem and leaf plot**
- Describing **range, median, mode, outliers, clusters,** and **gaps**
- Interpreting a back-to-back and a **split stem and leaf plot**

Materials/Resources

- Trash cans of the same size (one per five students)
- Yardstick
- Masking tape
- Scrap paper, 8.5" × 11" (from recycling bin)
- Blackline Master 23, **Tally Sheet for Trashball Hoops,** page 100 (one per student)
- Ready Reference 8, **Split Stem and Leaf Plots,** page 129
- Ready Reference 9, **Back-to-Back Stem and Leaf Plots,** page 130

Understanding the Problem

Display the transparency. Use these questions to facilitate discussion.

➤ Do trashballers show similar performance with both shooting hands? [To answer the question, we will collect two sets of data.]

➤ Is one hand more accurate than the other? [We need a method of comparing two sets of data.]

➤ Which hand will be more accurate? The dominant (writing) hand or the other? [Expect the dominant hand generally.]

➤ How can we display data of students' performances as trashballers? [We could construct a back-to-back stem and leaf plot.]

How Many Hoops Can You Make?

You are the millionaire owner of the Detroit Dribblers of the National Trashball Association (NTA). Last season you dribbled your way into last place, but next week you get first choice in the draft!

You will scout for shooting talent and collect data on your players. How can you collect and use data to determine which trashball players have the best shooting records?

TEACHING THE INVESTIGATION

Gathering and Organizing the Data

Place each trash can next to a wall. From the edge of the trash can, measure 8 feet and make a shooting line on the floor with a strip of tape. Crumple pieces of $8\frac{1}{2}" \times 11"$ scrap paper to form trashballs and have them available near each trash can.

Students will choose partners and bring the tally sheet and 5 trashballs to an open court. Before shooting, students predict the number of baskets in 20 shots that they will make with each hand. Direct students to stand behind the shooting line and take 20 shots, 5 at a time, with each hand. Have them record the number of successful baskets in a frequency table. These 20 shots can be thought of as a sample of their performance as a trashballer. (Students may want to take 5 practice shots.)

For Primary Students:

Students can display the data collected in a line plot or bar graph. The distance between the shooting line and the trash can may need to be adjusted.

For Intermediate Students:

On the chalkboard, have students construct a stem and leaf plot of the data collected from everyone in the class. Explain how to make a **split stem and leaf plot** when the data have a great many leaves for each stem. Use Ready Reference 8, page 129. The data may resemble the split stem and leaf plots shown above.

Number of Baskets Made with Non-writing Hand

```
0 |  0 3 3 3 4 4 4 4
• |  5 5 5 5 6 8 9 9
1 |  0 0 1 2
```

Number of Baskets Made with Writing Hand

```
0 |  0 0 1 3 3 3
• |  5 5 5 5 6 8 8 9
1 |  0 0 2 3 3
• |  5        Key:  0 | 4 = 4 strokes
                    • | 5 = 5 strokes
                 (• is the same value as
                 the stem above it, with a
                 leaf value of 5–9)
```

To compare the two data sets, construct a **back-to-back stem and leaf plot.** The data in the set on the right (with writing hand) remains the same. The data in the set on the left (with non-writing hand) is placed on the plot re-using the center stem and listing the leaves right-to-left. The two data sets can then be compared easily for symmetry, shifting of data, and so on.

Number of Baskets Made with Non-writing Hand		Number of Baskets Made with Writing Hand
4 4 4 4 3 3 3 0	0	0 0 1 3 3 3
9 9 8 6 5 5 5 5	•	5 5 5 5 6 8 8 9
2 1 0 0	1	0 0 2 3 3
	•	5
0 |1| = 10 baskets		|1| 0 = 10 baskets

Describing and Interpreting the Data

These questions can help students analyze their findings as they begin to formulate a solution.

Describe the data collected on the trashball shooting performance of the group using the terms **range, median, mode, outlier, clusters,** and **gaps**.

➤ How did the predictions compare to actual performance? [Predictions were higher or lower than the actual performance.]

➤ Based on our sample, can we determine whether the performances of both shooting hands are equal? different? significantly different?

➤ If a larger sample was taken, what do you predict would happen?

➤ How could we determine if the distance from the shooting line to the trash can has an impact on the results? [Make the distance longer or shorter and construct a back-to-back stem and leaf plot of the results of one shooting hand to compare the data.]

Drawing Conclusions

These questions can help students describe their solutions.

➤ How does the rewriting of the stem and leaf plots as a back-to-back stem and leaf plot help in the interpretation of data? [It enables you to look at two sets of data and compare the shape of the data and the shifting of the data.]

➤ How would a stem and leaf plot representing a small range of data affect our ability to draw conclusions? [If everyone has the same relative score, there is no discernible difference in ability. A larger set of data needs to be collected.]

➤ What do you do with trashballs after they wear out? [Recycle them!]

Additional Investigations and Projects

➤ Construct a back-to-back stem and leaf plot comparing the predicted number of baskets to the actual number of baskets made with the dominant (writing) hand.

➤ Conduct the same experiment varying the distance between the trash can and the shooting line or recording the number of successful shots within a given time limit.

➤ Conduct the trashball experiment increasing the sample size to 40 shots.

Tally Sheet for Trashball Hoops

Predict how many baskets you will make with each hand.

I will make _____ out of 20 tosses with my non-writing hand. That is my _____ hand.

I will make _____ out of 20 tosses with my writing hand. That is my _____ hand.

Work with a partner. Take turns tossing 5 trashballs, first with your non-writing hand, then with your writing hand. Your partner will tally the number of baskets you make. Keep going until both of you have made 20 tosses with each hand.

Keep accurate records. Your totals will be compiled in a graph of the class results.

My Non-writing Hand	Tosses	My Writing Hand
	5	
	5	
	5	
	5	
Total Baskets = _____	20	Total Baskets = _____

EQL INVESTIGATION 16

Popcorn Projectiles

INVESTIGATION OVERVIEW

Statistical Ideas

- Finding **mean** and **median**
- Constructing and interpreting **line plots** and **stem and leaf plots**
- Measuring to the nearest centimeter/inch

Materials/Resources

- Hot air popcorn popper or hot plate and sauce pan
- Popcorn, tablespoon, yardsticks, rulers, tape measures
- Landing field (bulletin board paper, drop cloth, plastic table cloth, or tile floor)
- Ready Reference 7, **Stem and Leaf Plots**, pages 127–128
- Ready Reference 8, **Split Stem and Leaf Plots**, page 129

Understanding the Problem

Display the transparency. Use these questions to facilitate discussion.

➤ How can we collect the data? What procedures should we use? [We might construct a popcorn landing field.]

➤ Should we measure from the center or edge of the popper? [The group decides. The popper can be removed and its position can be marked.]

➤ Are we measuring popped kernels only? [Intermediate students may take a second set of measurements on the unpopped kernels to use later.]

➤ How do we measure the distances without disturbing the data? [Students may need to remove shoes, work in pairs, take turns, and so on.]

How Far Will the Popcorn Travel?

As Colonel Wright started to make some popcorn, the telephone rang in the next room. She plugged in the popper and then answered the telephone. When she returned, popcorn was everywhere. She had forgotten to put the lid on the popper!

➤ How far would a piece of popcorn travel?

➤ What is the average popcorn flight?

Gathering and Organizing the Data

For Intermediate Students:

The landing field for this activity should be marked off ahead of time into 6 equal pie shaped sections. (Masking tape on the floor works nicely.) Assign 1 group per section to count and measure the distance the popcorn flies.

Students should sit outside the section until the popcorn is popped. Place the open popper in the center, turn it on to warm up, and then add one tablespoon of corn kernels. Allow the popcorn to pop. Have each group measure the distance each piece flew and remove each piece from the landing area as soon as its landing distance has been measured.

✪ Be sure to check the corn popper to make sure the popper will throw the kernels. Some popcorn popper models will not work for this investigation. The short-neck models usually work better.

Another alternative to using a corn popper is using a small pot and a hot plate. Place a small amount of oil in the pot to coat the bottom. Place the kernels in the pot and move children away from the area for safety reasons. Flying unpopped kernels could cause injury.

When all measurements are completed, encourage students to discuss with their teammates how the data for the popped kernels might be shown on a line plot. [Chart paper cut lengthwise and taped end-to-end can be used to make a larger line plot. For example, given the data below, construct a line plot and stem and leaf plot.]

31, 5, 14, 28, 9, 1, 42, 39, 11, 24, 35, 19, 2, 23, 6, 13, 2, 20, 14, 8, 15, 47, 23, 15, 3, 26, 19, 11, 7, 4, 42, 18, 37, 2, 30, 8, 25, 16, 40, 6, 14, 38, 5, 32, 51, 33, 13, 21, 14, 2, 13, 30, 12, 15, 31, 8, 3, 11

Landing Distances (cm)

0	1 2 2 2 3 3 4
•	5 5 6 6 7 8 8 8 9
1	1 1 1 2 3 3 3 4 4 4 4
•	5 5 5 6 8 9 9
2	0 1 3 3 4
•	5 6 8
3	0 0 1 1 2 3
•	5 7 8 9
4	0 2 2
•	7
5	1

Key: 1|1 = 11 cm

Flight of Popcorn

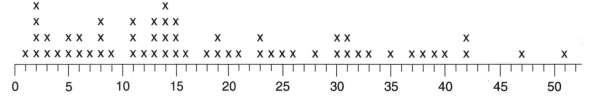

For Primary Students:

The landing area may consist of concentric circles drawn around the popcorn popper on a floor mat. Students may tally the number of pieces of popcorn that land in each of the concentric circles. The circles may be colored or labeled with letters for easy identification. This type of landing field can be reused.

Another possibility is that once the popcorn is popped, each piece of popcorn is picked up and replaced by a self-stick dot or a mark made with magic marker. After the popcorn placement is marked, students can walk about without disturbing the data. They can use tape measures to gain measuring experience. The mat can be saved to use over a period of several days.

Describing and Interpreting the Data

These questions can help students analyze their findings as they formulate a solution.

➤ Look at the two different representations of data. What information can you learn from each display? [A line plot shows the range of the data and how the data is distributed over that range. The stem and leaf plot enables us to see clusters that appear over a large range.]

➤ What are the advantages or disadvantages of each display? [In the case of a large set of data, the line plot can be time consuming in its construction. The stem and leaf plot is quick, efficient, takes up less space, and can be interpreted rapidly.]

➤ What is the shape of the data? Which displays have clusters, outliers, and gaps?

➤ Find the **mean** and **median** for each display. Is one of these a better summary for this set of data? [Both the mean and median summarize the data by giving a measure of the center of the data values. The median generally gives a more reasonable summary since it is not affected by a few extreme values. When there are no outliers, there will generally not be much difference between the mean and median, so what we choose won't matter.]

➤ Discuss the relationship between the mean and median for skewed data and symmetric data. [When the data is symmetric, approximately equal numbers of values lie left of the center as right of the center. When data is skewed, the values are distributed in a long tail stretching in one direction away from the main cluster of values. The arithmetic mean will be located away from the median value because the extremes and outliers will affect the calculation of the mean.]

Drawing Conclusions

These questions can help students describe their solutions.

➤ Based on the measurements, what generalizations can be made about the flight of popcorn when the lid is left off the popper?

➤ Is the mean or median a better summary number for this data?

➤ Which graphical representation of the data gives you the most information about the data that was gathered?

Additional Investigations and Projects

Repeat the experiment changing one variable or measuring another outcome.

➤ Use another brand of popcorn. Are the distances the same or different?

➤ Pop more or less than 1 tablespoon of popcorn. Are there any noticeable differences from the first set of data collected?

➤ Change the type of popcorn popper. How does that affect the data?

➤ Use yarn to make a landing field with concentric circles. Are there any symmetrical patterns? Is the popcorn evenly distributed around the circle?

➤ When the popcorn is popped, many of the kernels do not pop. Measure the flight distance of the unpopped kernels. Record the data and display the data in a stem and leaf plot or histogram. You could also make a back-to-back stem and leaf plot comparing the flight distances of popped and unpopped kernels.

A TV for Sara

INVESTIGATION OVERVIEW

Statistical Ideas

- **Plotting points** on a **coordinate grid**
- Using the **number line**
- Constructing and interpreting a **scatter plot**
- Observing a **trend** or **association**

Materials/Resources

- A coordinate grid on chart paper or an overhead transparency grid and overhead pen (one per group)
- A sheet of sticky dots (enough for each student)
- Blackline Master 24, **TV, or Not TV, That is the Question,** page 112 (one per student)
- Ready Reference 10, **Scatter Plots,** pages 131–133

Understanding the Problem

Display the transparency. Use these questions to facilitate discussion.

➤ What is a typical number of television sets in a family of Sara's size? How can we find out? [Sample a group or use a resource like the census or an almanac.]

➤ As we count the number of people in the household, are there members who shouldn't be counted? (Do we count a brother away at college?)

➤ Should a broken TV set be included in the data? [Group discussion will include a variety of opinions, but a consensus should be reached.]

Will Sara Get her TV?

Sara wants her own TV for her birthday. She says that all her friends have their own television sets, but her mother disagrees. She says one set is enough for four people.

➤ Do you think Sara's family should buy another television set?

➤ What reasons might Sara give to persuade her mother to buy another TV set?

➤ What reasons might Sara's mother have for not buying another TV?

TEACHING THE INVESTIGATION

Gathering and Organizing the Data

To collect and graph the student data, choose one of the following methods for constructing a scatter plot. A **scatter plot** is a graph that shows a set of points (ordered pairs), based on two sets of data plotted on a **coordinate grid**.

For Intermediate Students:

Method 1: Have each student record the number of TVs and people in their household on a slip of paper labeled with two columns, "TVs" and "Household Members." These slips can be collected in a shoe box, and a sample number of responses can be selected and graphed using an overhead transparency grid.

Method 2: Do the graphing activity in groups. Each group will receive an overhead transparency grid with horizontal axis labeled "People in the household" and vertical axis labeled "TVs in the house," as in the example below. Each student can locate the point for his or her own data on the transparency. Groups can then overlap transparent grids on the overhead projector to display the total class data.

For Primary Students:

Method 3: Display a chart paper coordinate grid. Call on students to represent their data by placing a self-stick dot on the grid. Assist

them in reading the two directions simultaneously. Help them read and understand the placement of points.

Ask students interpretive questions about their scatter plot, such as:

➤ How many households have 2 people, 3 people, 4 people, and so on?

➤ How many households have 1 TV, 2 TVs, and so on?

➤ How many households of 2 people have 1 TV, 2 TVs, 3 TVs, and so on?

➤ How many data points are illustrated on this scatter plot? [9]

➤ If we have several points occupying the same area, how can we represent them? [Cluster them around the point.]

➤ How many people owned two or more TVs? [The answer will include the number of people who owned 2, 3, 4, 5 TVs, and so on.]

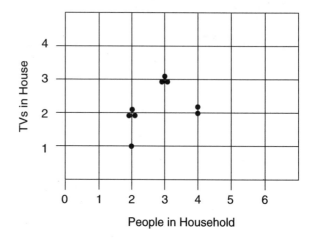

Describing and Interpreting the Data

Using the data on the scatter plot on the class chart or transparency, ask questions that lead students to become comfortable with statistical vocabulary.

➤ Which household has the most people? Describe how you know.

➤ Which household has the most televisions? Describe how you know.

➤ Is there a relationship between the number of people and the number of TVs? [An **association** is the word that describes a strong connection between two sets of data. Students should be able to see a pattern in the data. For example, as the number of people in the household increases, the number of televisions may also increase. However, a much larger data set must be used before stating that an association exists.]

Drawing Conclusions

Have the students discuss patterns in their graph.

Students might sketch a line showing the pattern. To develop the formal concept of a **trend line**, pose questions like the following:

➤ Suppose we had a situation in which every person in a household had one TV (that is, 1 TV for 1 person, 2 TVs for 2 peo-

ple, 5 TVs for 5 people, and so on). Where would these points be located on the scatter plot? [They would be in a straight line, ascending at a 45 degree angle, from left to right. If a point falls on the line, the number of TVs matches the number of people ($x = y$ line). If the point falls below the line, there are fewer TVs than people; above the line, there are more TVs than people.]

Direct the students to complete TV, or Not TV, That is the Question, to assess their understanding.

Additional Investigations and Projects

➤ Count the number of clocks and watches in your house and the number of people. Combine your data with that of other students and make a scatter plot. What trend or association do you notice?

➤ Survey the class for the following information: number of hours per night watching TV and number of hours per night doing homework. Then graph the class results on a scatter plot.

➤ Make a math connection to a conservation unit by surveying and graphing the daily water meter reading or electricity consumption and the number of people in a family.

TV, or Not TV, That is the Question

1. Use the data from your scatter plot to write a note to Sara. Tell her about any trends, clusters, gaps, and outliers that you have observed. Write the note on the back of this sheet of paper.

2. Sara still hopes to get a TV for her birthday. Her class made the scatter plot below. Write a letter to Sara's family to try to persuade them to buy another TV. Use the information shown on the scatter plot to support your opinion. (Use the correct letter form on a clean sheet of paper.)

Number of People and Televisions per Household in Sara's 5th Grade Class

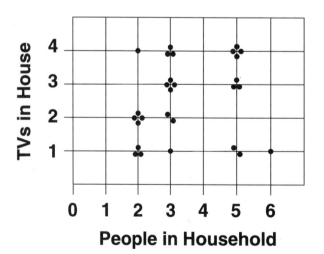

Strings and Swings

INVESTIGATION OVERVIEW

Statistical Ideas

- Constructing a **scatter plot**
- Discussing the use of **mode, median,** and **mean**
- Describing **association** and **correlation**

Materials/Resources

Per group of three students:

- Graph paper (hundreds chart paper works well)
- $\frac{1}{2}$" washer tied to a string, cut to a specific length, and placed in an envelope labeled with the string length (see page 116)
- Ready Reference 10, **Scatter Plots,** pages 131–133

For the entire class:

- Class chart and large-sized coordinate grid

Understanding the Problem

Display the transparency. Use these questions to facilitate discussion.

➤ When you put a pendulum into motion, the swing is dependent upon several variables. What are some of these variables? [keeping hands steady, starting the swing at the same point each time, air movement in the room, keeping time carefully, and counting swings accurately, and so on]

➤ How will you count swings? [To avoid fractions, a swing will consist of a movement from right to left or left to right.] Would a scatter plot be helpful to compare the length of strings with the number of swings? [When two measurements are taken, the measurements are paired as ordered pairs and the points can be plotted on a coordinate grid. You can then look for a pattern.]

Does the Length of a Pendulum's String Affect Its Swings?

William visited the Museum of American History in Washington, D.C., and was fascinated by the giant pendulum swinging from the ceiling. He began to experiment with pendulums when he returned home. He was curious about whether the length of the string had any relationship to the number of swings that the pendulum would make in 15 seconds. Do you think there is a relationship? How could you investigate this problem?

TEACHING THE INVESTIGATION

Gathering and Organizing the Data

Preparation:

To prepare a set of pendulums for the class, cut strings and tie them to $\frac{1}{2}$-inch washers. The string lengths need to be cut in increments of 10 centimeters, starting with 10 centimeters and going up to approximately 80 centimeters. Depending on class size, there may be some duplicate string lengths.

For Intermediate Students:

Divide the class into groups of three. Explain that one student will hold the pendulum, one will count the swings, and one will say "start" and time the 15-second interval, then say "stop." The team will record the count, and then team members will change roles. In this way, three different counts are recorded per team.

Distribute a pendulum to each group. Explain that it is important to explore how to measure the pendulum swings before beginning the experiment.

Allow one trial per group member, then record the counts on the board and discuss the differences found within each group and from group to group. Ask: Were we all holding the pendulums in the same way? What kind of inaccuracy could occur with the timing, and so on? Allow students to make conjectures concerning inconsistent measurements. All groups need to be consistent in taking any measurements, as it will greatly affect the data. Elicit students' ideas that lead to making the data collection uniform.

Encourage students holding the pendulum to extend both arms at shoulder height, parallel to the floor, holding the end of the string in one hand and the washer in the other. To start, students should simply release the washer from their fingers without applying any force or push to the washer. After releasing the washer, they can support the arm holding the pendulum with the other hand so that no "sympathetic" movement is added to the swing.

Remind students about what constitutes one swing of the pendulum. The student holding the pendulum should release it promptly with the word "start," and the student counting the number of swings should stop counting promptly with the word "stop."

Direct the teams to begin the 3 tests that will be their part of the experiment. Have students share their results and display them on a chart at the front of the room.

String Length	Number of Swings		
10	18	18	20
20	15	16	16
30	15	15	15
40	11	12	12
50	12	10	10
60	9	10	8
70	8	9	8
80	7	7	8

Direct students to discuss in their groups the number that best describes their pendulum swings. Have each group announce their number choice; tell whether it is the mean, median, or mode; and explain the reasoning for their choice. [If it is the number that occurred most often, it is the mode. If it is the number between the highest and lowest valves, it is the median. If the swings were added and divided by three, it is the mean.]

Using the data on the class chart, have students make a **scatter plot.** Put the string length on the horizontal axis (x-axis) and the number of swings on the vertical axis (y-axis). Plot the ordered pairs (string length, number of swings).

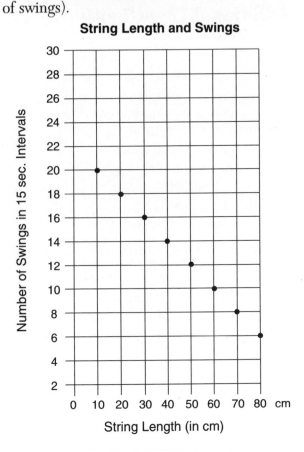

String Length and Swings

Number of Swings in 15 sec. Intervals

String Length (in cm)

For Primary Students:

Divide the class into pairs and distribute a pendulum to each pair. Explain the role of the person holding the pendulum and let these students practice. Explain the role of the person who is counting and let these students practice. Switch roles and practice. As soon as every pair is ready, you will say "start" and students will begin the experiment. After 15 seconds you will say "stop" and students will record the number of swings on a piece of scrap paper. You may need to discuss what should be done about incomplete swings when you called time. Have each pair repeat the same procedure for two trials, resulting in four measurements per pendulum. As a class, select the best measurement per pendulum and explain the reasoning. Circle it. Construct a class-sized scatter plot together. Look for patterns.

Describing and Interpreting the Data

These questions can help students analyze their findings as they begin to formulate solutions.

➤ What was the advantage in taking three trials (or more) and selecting the best measure? (Discuss **median** or **mode** if appropriate.) [More trials help data to be more accurate.]

➤ Would it have been better to find the **mean** of the three trials? [If the measurements are all close, the mean will work. An inaccurate measurement that is low or high may affect the data.]

➤ Have students examine the scatter plot and comment on any observations that they may note. Lead them to make statements that show there is an **association** between the length of strings and the number of swings.

Ask: Do there seem to be any trends or associations between the number of swings and the length of the pendulum strings? [They should include statements such as: "The longer the strings, the fewer the swings. The shorter the string, the more it swings."]

Ask: Can shortening the string cause the pendulum to swing more? (Demonstrate by swinging the 80 cm string, and then by pinching it in half and swinging it. Have students describe what they see.)

Drawing Conclusions

These questions and activities can help students describe their solutions.

➤ What general conclusions can you draw from this scatter plot? [A longer string will make fewer swings than a shorter string.]

➤ The Dutch scientist Christian Huygens patented the first pendulum clock in 1657. Write a letter to Mr. Huygen's great-grandchildren telling them what you learned about pendulums from this experiment.

➤ There is a famous saying, "A picture is worth a thousand words." How might this statement pertain to the visual representation of data that we used in this problem? How did the scatter plot help us to make observations about pendulums? [The scatter plot helped us to see the association between the string length and the number of swings in a given time.]

➤ If you were going to make a pendulum with a 100-centimeter string, predict the number of swings that it would make in 15 seconds. [Answers would be a few swings less than the number for the 80-cm string.]

Additional Investigations and Projects

➤ Use an almanac to gather data about average rainfall and temperatures in key American cities or world cities. Plot the data on a scatter plot to note any trends or associations.

➤ Research the distance of each planet from the sun. Also find the average daytime temperature on the planet. Use a scatter plot to display the data.

➤ Find the pulse rates of people of a variety of ages, for example, infants, 5 year olds, 10 year olds, 15 year olds, and adults. Make a scatter plot for the age of a person and number of heartbeats per minute.

EQL READY REFERENCE PAGES

A Problem-Solving Approach to Investigating Data

State the Problem

What is the question? Do we clearly understand all parts of the problem? Are there other ways to approach this problem?

Understand the Problem

Does the solution require counting or measuring? Do we need to define a step-by-step approach? Do we need to establish procedures that all investigators will follow so data is standardized?

Gather and Organize the Data

How can we gather the data? How can we represent the data? How can we best record the data? What materials will we need?

Describe and Interpret the Data

How can we describe patterns in the data? How can we interpret the data? What generalizations can we make? Is there more than one correct answer? Can the calculator or computer assist in the analysis of our data?

Draw Conclusions

Have we answered our original question? Would another form of graph have illustrated the data more clearly? Do we have a new question as a result of this investigation?

Try Other Investigations

If we sampled another group, or collected data in another way, would we expect the results to be similar?

Line Plots

A line plot is a graph that indicates the location of data points along a segment of the real number line.

The Problem:

Mia's friends like to play miniature golf. She had never played before. She borrowed a golf ball and golf club and practiced in her front yard. She marked a starting line and counted the number of strokes it took her to reach the hole.

Look at her data and the line plot. What story can you tell about Mia's first practice?

Follow these steps to make a line plot.

Step 1 Find the smallest and largest values in the data set.

Step 2 Draw a number line that includes these values. Be sure the number line extends past the smallest and largest values.

Step 3 Label the scale. Place a mark (usually an X or a dot) on the real number line that represents each data point.

Step 4 Title the graph.

Step 5 Look for patterns in the data and make statements about the data set.

Data Set

18, 17, 17, 16, 17, 13, 14, 16,
15, 13, 14, 13, 14, 9, 9, 13, 8

Mia's First Practice

```
                        X
                        X     X              X
            X           X     X        X     X
      X     X           X     X   X    X     X     X
  ─────────────────────────────────────────────────────
    7   8   9   10  11  12  13  14  15  16  17  18  19
                        strokes
```

Pictographs

A pictograph uses a repeated picture or symbol, in bar graph form, to represent data. The key tells the value of one symbol. The symbols compare quantity of a single variable. Addition (or multiplication) is used to find total amounts. Partial symbols can be used, but should be easy to identify and enable rapid calculation.

Step 1 Determine the value for each symbol. (The differences between categories will determine if the values will be to the nearest tens, hundreds, thousands, and so on.)

Step 2 Determine whether a fractional part of a symbol will be used. It is best to use pictures that are quick and easy to interpret. Dividing pictures in thirds or smaller can be misleading.

Step 3 Label the key.

Step 4 Give the pictograph a specific title.

Fabric Squares
Attribute: Texture

Texture		
Stiff	🖐🖐🖐🖐🖐🖐🖐🖐🖐🖐🖐	
Nubby	🖐🖐	
Smooth	🖐🖐🖐🖐	

🖐 = 2 pieces of cloth

Glyphs

A glyph, as in *hieroglyphic*, is a picture that graphically represents data that includes several variables. Each symbol of the picture represents a different variable and has degrees of variation that represent proportion for quantifying within that variable.

Step 1 Select a picture that relates symbolically to the data.

Example: A survey of student recreational preferences might have a facial glyph with eyes for time spent reading, ears for time on the phone, mouth for talking or being with friends, hat for playing sports, and so on.

Example: Data from bodies of water might be represented by a fish shape with eyes for water clarity (turbidity), gills for dissolved oxygen level, fins for pH level, and so on.

Step 2 Each symbol might be drawn proportionally larger (or smaller) to represent greater (or lesser) values.

Step 3 A key should indicate the symbol being used and the coding or enlarging that stands for each interval measurement. Use a title if appropriate.

Watching TV

Time spent (minutes)	60 or less	61–120	121–180	181 or more
Symbol (eyes)	○ ○	● ●	◎ ◎	◉ ◉

Listening to music

Time spent (minutes)	30 or less	31–60	61–90	91 or more
Symbol (ears)	( )	(( ))	((( )))	(((( ))))

Talking on telephone

Time spent (minutes)	15 or less	16–30	31–45	46 or more
Symbol (mouth)	—	⌐	⌣	⊂⊃

Bar Graphs

A bar graph uses parallel bars, either horizontal or vertical, to represent counts for several categories. One bar is used for each category with the length of the bar representing the count for that category. Sometimes the length of the bar represents the percentage of the total count that falls in that category.

The Problem:

Third-grade students are planning a pizza party and want to know which pizza toppings to order. The special price rate only allows them to choose 2 different pizza toppings. They took a survey of the 82 students and the results are listed below. Examine the data and the bar graph. Which two pizza toppings should they order?

Data Set

Extra cheese: 31   Sausage: 7
Pepperoni: 43   Green pepper: 1

Follow these steps to make a bar graph.

Step 1 There will be two axes; the horizontal axis (*x*-axis) displays the individual categories.

Step 2 The vertical axis (*y*-axis) contains the scale. Label the scale.

Step 3 Construct one bar per category on the *x*-axis with the length of the bar equal to the count for the category. Give the graph a **title.**

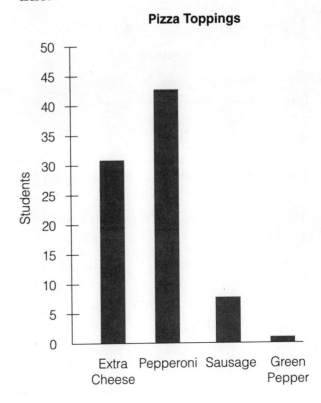

Pizza Toppings

Probability

Probability is a measure of how likely an event is to occur.

Probability can be determined experimentally—gathering and recording the relative frequency of event occurrences. This method becomes more reliable as more trials are run.

Probability can be determined theoretically—by thinking about the rules that govern the occurrences of events.

Flipping a coin: $P(H) = \frac{1}{2}$ or $P(T) = \frac{1}{2}$

Probability Scale

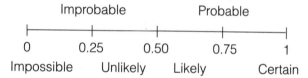

Probability language: If the probability is $\frac{1}{2}$, you can say:

There is a 1 in 2 chance.	There is a 1 out of 2 chance.
The odds are 50-50.	The results are in our favor 50% of the time.

There is a 0.5 chance.

Expressing possible outcomes:

Example: When rolling two dice, what are the possible outcomes?

Sample Space

1,1	1,2	1,3	1,4	1,5	1,6
2,1	2,2	2,3	2,4	2,5	2,6
3,1	3,2	3,3	3,4	3,5	3,6
4,1	4,2	4,3	4,4	4,5	4,6
5,1	5,2	5,3	5,4	5,5	5,6
6,1	6,2	6,3	6,4	6,5	6,6

Matrix (of sums of 2 dice)

	1	2	3	4	5	6
1	2	3	4	5	6	7
2	3	4	5	6	7	8
3	4	5	6	7	8	9
4	5	6	7	8	9	10
5	6	7	8	9	10	11
6	7	8	9	10	11	12

Tree Diagrams

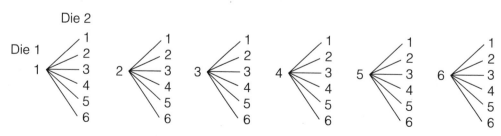

Simulation: A Probability Experiment

Probability arises out of a need to anticipate what might happen in a random event that has not yet occurred. What is the probability that our favorite football team will win the coin toss at the start of the game? What is the probability that they will win the game?

Some of these probabilities can be answered by theoretical arguments. However, many require empirical arguments, that is, data is collected by actually doing the event in question or by a simulation (model) of an actual event.

The Problem

Carla had five minutes remaining to complete a multiple-choice test, and still had 10 unanswered questions. She decided to guess the answers to these questions. Each question had four choices all of which seemed reasonable. What is the probability that she will get 5 of these 10 answers correct? How many questions is she most likely to get correct?

Follow these steps to act out a simulation.

Step 1 State the problem clearly.

What is the probability that Carla will guess 5 out of the 10 questions correctly when her guesses are at random?

Step 2 Define the key component (the single activity that will be repeated a number of times in the simulation).

The key activity is guessing at random an answer to an individual question.

Step 3 State the problem assumptions and predict the probability.

We have to assume that Carla will not look for patterns when she is guessing her answers. In this case, the probability of guessing a single correct answer is 25% or $\frac{1}{4}$. The probability of answering 5 out of 10 questions correctly is a different probability question.

Step 4 Select a model.

Model 1

Four colored chips (1 green and 3 red) could be placed in a cup and one could be drawn at random. If a green chip is drawn, the question was answered correctly. If a red chip is drawn, the question was answered incorrectly.

Model 2

A die could be thrown. If a one appears, the question was answered correctly. If a 2, 3, or 4 appears, the question was answered incorrectly. If a 5 or a 6 appears, disregard and repeat the throw.

Model 3

A spinner with four regions could be used. Designate which region represents the correct answer and the three remaining regions will represent incorrect responses.

Step 5 Define and conduct a trial.

A trial is determined by the number of times the key component must be performed to complete the entire activity.

We will need to simulate 10 test questions being answered at random, to complete one trial. Using the chips as a model, a chip must be selected from the cup, and the result recorded (simulating a correct answer or incorrect answer). Repeat this procedure nine more times to complete the trial.

Step 6 Record observations.

Records should show the number of correctly answered questions for each trial.

Step 7 Repeat steps 5 and 6.
The activity should be repeated as time will allow. The more trials recorded, the more accurate the results will be.

Step 8 Summarize results.

The probability of randomly answering 5 out of 10 questions correctly is found by taking the total number of favorable outcomes and dividing by the total number of trials.

A favorable outcome for Carla's test problem is where the correct response was chosen at least 5 out of 10 times.

READY REFERENCE 7

Stem and Leaf Plots

Data covering a range of 25 numbers or more on the real number line might appear crowded on a line plot, making it difficult to recover the exact numerical values. A stem and leaf plot allows us to list the exact values in a meaningful array.

The Problem

Mia's group at summer camp played miniature golf one afternoon. Before the game, Mia was a little worried because she had never played a whole game before; but she thought she would do all right.

The Data Set shows the scores of all who played. Her score was 35. How did she do? Was she in the top 25%? top 50%? lower 50%? lower 25%?

Data Set
26, 30, 40, 31, 35, 32, 25, 39, 31, 54, 24,
35, 46, 36, 48, 40, 37, 38, 41, 33, 37, 33, 37

Follow these steps to make a stem and leaf plot.

Step 1 Find the smallest and largest values. (The smallest value is 24 and the largest is 54.)

Step 2 Because the smallest value, 24, has a 2 in the tens place and the largest value, 54, has a 5 in the tens place, the stems will be the digits 2 to 5. Write these stems vertically with a line to the right.

```
2 |
3 |
4 |
5 |
```

Step 3 Separate each value into the stem and leaf. (Digits in the tens place are listed vertically and digits in the ones place are listed horizontally.) The first value is 26. Its stem is 2 and its leaf is 6. It is placed on the plot as follows:

```
2 | 6
3 |
4 |
5 |
```

Continue until all the values are listed on the plot. Be sure to keep the numbers evenly spaced and lined up in columns. (Graph paper may be used to help keep the proper spacing.)

```
2 | 6 5 4
3 | 0 1 5 2 9 1 5 6 7 8 3 7 3 7
4 | 0 6 8 0 1
5 | 4
```

EQL Ready Reference Pages   127

Step 4 On a new plot, arrange the leaves so they are in order from the smallest value to largest value. This makes identification of median and mode more apparent. Be sure to include a title and a key or explanation of the stem and leaf plot.

Miniature Golf Scores

```
2 | 4 5 6
3 | 0 1 1 2 3 3 5 5 6 7 7 7 8 9
4 | 0 0 1 6 8
5 | 4
```
Key: 2|4 =
24 strokes

Step 5 Locate the median. The median splits the data in half (36). Locate the median for each of the halves. This divides the data set into quarters, or quartiles (lower half 31, upper half 40).

Miniature Golf Scores

```
2 | 4 5 6
3 | 0 1 1 2 3 3 5 5 [6] 7 7 7 8 9
4 | 0 0 1 6 8
5 | 4
```
Key: 2|4 =
24 strokes

Step 6 Describe and interpret the data. Use these terms to describe the shape of the data: *range, cluster, gaps, distribution* (symmetric or not?)
Use these terms to summarize the data: *mode, median, mean*

Split Stem and Leaf Plots

When a stem and leaf plot is constructed and has a high number of leaves per stem, the stem may be split so that the data may be spread out to make patterns in the distribution easier to see.

Data set: Summer campers miniature golf scores

24, 25, 26, 30, 31, 31, 32, 33, 33, 35, 35, 36, 37, 37, 37, 38, 39, 40, 40, 41, 46, 48, 54

Follow these steps to make a split stem and leaf plot.

Step 1 For each value placed on the stem, insert a point between the digits. This indicates that the value above it is repeated in the line it occupies.

```
2
•
3
•
4
•
5
```

Step 2 Each stem now occupies two lines. All the leaves with values from 0–4 will be listed on the first stem. All the leaves with values 5–9 will be listed on the second stem, (point).

Miniature Golf Scores

```
2 | 4
• | 5 6
3 | 0 1 1 2 3 3
• | 5 5 6 7 7 7 8 9
4 | 0 0 1
• | 6 8
5 | 4
```

Key: 2|4 = 24 strokes
  •|5 = 25 strokes
(• is the same value as the stem above it, with a leaf value of 5–9)

Step 3 Add a title and key. Define the point symbol in the key.

Back-to-Back Stem and Leaf Plots

To compare the data displayed on two stem and leaf plots, it is easier to view and compare distributions when they share the same scale. The two data sets can be constructed on the same stem.

Data Sets

Golf Scores from Day 2	Golf Scores from Day 1
22, 23, 23, 25, 25, 26,	24, 25, 26, 30, 31, 31
28, 29, 30, 30, 31, 32,	32, 33, 33, 35, 35, 36,
33, 33, 34, 34, 34, 37,	37, 37, 37, 38, 39, 40,
38, 39, 40, 41, 46	40, 41, 46, 48, 54

Follow these steps to make a back-to-back stem and leaf plot.

Step 1 Construct a stem and leaf plot using the first data set. Use a split stem and leaf plot if data sets are large.

Miniature Golf Scores from Day 1

Stem	Leaf
2	4
•	5 6
3	0 1 1 2 3 3
•	5 5 6 7 7 7 8 9
4	0 0 1
•	6 8
5	4

Step 2 Put the data from the second set in order.

Step 3 Place the data on the same stem and leaf plot, re-using the center stem, and listing the leaves right-to-left. The two data sets can be compared for symmetry. The shifting of data can be seen easily.

Miniature Golf Scores from Day 2	Stem	Miniature Golf Scores from Day 1
3 3 2	2	4
9 8 6 5 5	•	5 6
4 4 4 3 3 2 1 0 0	3	0 1 1 2 3 3
9 8 7	•	5 5 6 7 7 7 8 9
1 0	4	0 0 1
6	•	6 8
	5	4

Key: |2|4 = 24 strokes
3|2| = 23 strokes

READY REFERENCE 10

Scatter Plots

A **scatter plot** shows the relationship between paired measurements by plotting each ordered pair on a coordinate grid. The first number of the pair is marked off along the horizontal axis (or x-axis) and the second number is marked off along the vertical axis (or y-axis).

The Problem:

Each child in the kindergarten class was measured for height. Then each student's right foot was measured for length. Was there an association between the height of students and their foot length?

Data Set: (Height, Length of foot)

(98, 15) (99, 15) (100, 16) (100, 16)
(102, 16) (104, 18) (104, 18) (105, 18)
(105, 18) (105, 19) (105, 19) (106, 19)
(107, 19) (108, 20) (109, 20) (111, 21)
(113, 21) (115, 22)

Follow these steps to make a scatter plot.

Step 1 Select the intervals of measurement to be used on the x-axis and y-axis that best represent the data. Select graph paper appropriate to the range of measurements being represented.

Step 2 Construct the x-axis scale (horizontal scale), beginning with zero at the origin. If there is a considerable gap before the range of values in the data set, use a broken scale symbol (⎯〰). Be sure numbers are *not* placed in spaces, as in bar graph construction.

Step 3 Label the x-axis, indicating the scale in the label.

Step 4 Construct the y-axis scale, (vertical scale), beginning with zero at the origin. Determine whether the broken scale symbol will be used.

Step 5 Label the y-axis indicating the scale in the label.

Step 6 Each member of the data set has two measurements that are expressed as ordered pairs or coordinates. The first number in the ordered pair is located on the scale along the x-axis (horizontal axis); the second number is located on the scale along the y-axis (vertical axis). Each point should be plotted where the two lines intersect. Plot the points from the data set on the coordinate grid.

Step 7 Give the scatter plot a title.

Step 8 Interpret the data, noting and describing trends. Does the pattern of points indicate that an association exists?

EQL Ready Reference Pages 131

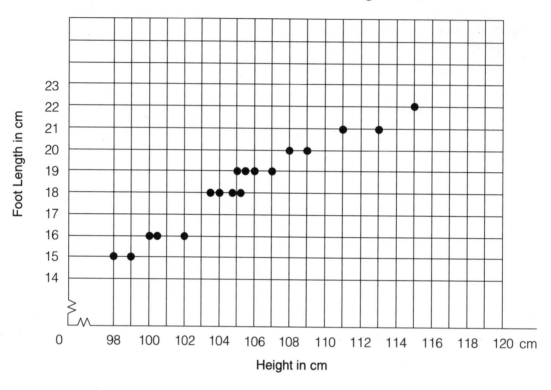

Comparing Height and Foot Size of Kindergarten Students

[In the example, the pattern in this graph shows the points are scattered in an upward slant to the right. This indicates a positive association. There is a link implied between the data on the *x*-axis and the data on the *y*-axis. The trend shows that those who are taller generally have longer feet.]

Patterns in scatter plots reflect the type and strength of the association between the two measured variables represented. When the points of a scatter plot lie along a straight line, the association between the variables is called linear and the strength of this association is measured by correlation.

The fact that two sets of measurements are correlated does not mean that one variable causes the other. Height is positively correlated with foot length, but the association between the two is caused by a third factor, growth of the person.

Figures 1 through 3: These figures show us no clear linear relationship between the variables.

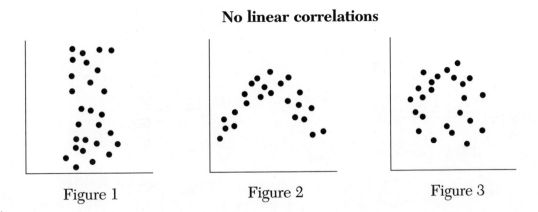

No linear correlations

Figure 1

Figure 2

Figure 3

Figures 4 through 7: These figures show us there is some relationship between two variables.

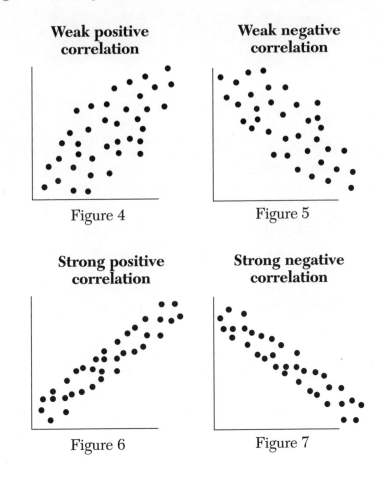

Weak positive correlation

Weak negative correlation

Figure 4

Figure 5

Strong positive correlation

Strong negative correlation

Figure 6

Figure 7

GLOSSARY

Association A trend in the data display indicating one set of measurements tends to rise or fall with another set of measurements. (See Ready Reference 10)

Axes The plural of "axis," which refers to both the horizontal axis and the vertical axis on a coordinate grid.

Back-to-back stem and leaf plot This is a variation of a stem and leaf plot. Two sets of data measuring similar outcomes can be placed on the same stem with leaves of one set of data to the right and leaves of one set of data to the left. It is helpful in comparing two data sets. (See Ready Reference 9)

Bar graph A graph of data with parallel bars for comparing information from several categories. Each bar represents a category. The height of the bar represents a numerical count. (See Ready Reference 4)

Broken scale symbol The broken scale symbol (‿ᶺ) may be used on either axis to indicate a gap exists from the origin to the first interval displayed on the scale. This conserves space and makes the graph easier to read.

Clusters and gaps Sometimes data piles up over groups of numbers on the number line, forming clusters. The spaces between the clusters are called gaps.

Coordinate grid A series of intersecting horizontal and vertical lines spaced at uniform intervals on which points are plotted.

Coordinates The ordered pair of numbers that indicate a point position on the horizontal and vertical axes of a coordinate grid.

Correlation A measure of association (closeness to a straight line) attached to data on scatter plots. (Note: Association or correlation is not the same as causality.)

Datum A single piece of data from a data set.

Distribution Data represented on a number line is distributed or spread out in some fashion. Sometimes it is stacked up in peaks; sometimes it is spread evenly. It may, for example, be mound-shaped or it may have two or three peaks. It may be U-shaped or J-shaped, or rectangular-shaped.

Event An outcome of a probability experiment.

Experiment The collecting of data through a planned activity.

Experimental probability Estimating the probability by observation of an event which is repeated in order to collect data on the relative frequency of an event's occurrence. (Also known as empirical probability.)

Frequency The number of times an occurrence takes place as expressed in a count. This count is referred to as a frequency.

Frequency table Paired columns that indicate the category being observed and the frequency (count or tally) of the occurrences for each category.

GLOSSARY

Glyph A glyph, as in *hieroglyphic*, is a picture that graphically represents data that includes several variables. Each symbol of the picture represents a different variable. The symbol should have degrees of variation that can represent proper proportion. (See Ready Reference 3)

Grid A series of horizontal and vertical lines at regular intervals that form a pattern like that used in graphing.

Interval The distance on a real number scale between two consecutive tick marks indicates the interval. Each space between the tick marks encompasses the number (or numbers) and all the fractional parts in that full range.

Line plot A graph that indicates the location of data along a segment of the real number line. (See Ready Reference 2)

Lower extreme The smallest value in the set of data is the lower extreme.

Lower quartile When the data set is ordered from the smallest to the largest values, the data set can be divided into four quarters. The numerical value that cuts off the lower quarter of data points is called the lower quartile.

Matrix A rectangular arrangement of numbers or symbols. (See Ready Reference 5)

Mean The arithmetic average of a set of measurements, computed by adding all the measurements, then dividing that sum by the number of measurements.

Median The measurement that lies in the middle after the measurements are put in order from smallest to largest. If there are two measurements in the middle, the median is the midpoint between the two. Half of the data points will be equal to or higher and half of the data points will be equal to or lower than the median. The median represents a type of center of the data set.

Mode The high point of a data distribution; it represents the data value or values that occur most often in the data set.

Negative association A pattern in the shape of the data that shows when one measurement grows larger, the second measurement grows smaller. An ellipse drawn around the data points, in a negative association, will be slanted upward to the left or downward to the right.

Ordered pairs The ordered pair of numbers that represents two measurements that will be indicated as one point on the coordinate grid.

Origin The point on a coordinate plane where the x-axis and the y-axis meet. The coordinates are (0,0).

Outcomes Any possible result of an activity or experiment. There are many ways to record outcomes. Results can be recorded on a **list**, in a **tree diagram,** or as a **matrix** or **array**, and so on.

Outlier The term can be used informally to describe any point (or points) that lies distant from the remainder of the data. (A technical definition of "outlier" is any point

GLOSSARY

that lies more than 1.5 inter-quartile ranges beyond the upper quartile or lower quartile.)

Pictograph A pictograph uses a repeat picture, in bar graph form, to represent data. The symbols compare quantity of a single variable. (See Ready Reference 3)

Positive association A pattern in the shape of the data that shows when one measurement grows larger, the second measurement grows larger. An ellipse drawn around the data points, in a positive association, will be slanted upward to the right.

Probability A measure of the likelihood that an event will occur. Probability arises out of a need to anticipate what might happen in a random event that has not yet occurred.

Proportional Maintaining a ratio when comparing two or more different quantities.

Quartile When data is ordered smallest to largest or largest to smallest, the median can be located and the data set can be subdivided into quarters or quartiles.

Range The difference between the largest value in the data set and the smallest value in the data set.

Rank Placing in numerical order according to scale or value.

Relative frequency The number of times an event occurs divided by the total number of trials.

Sample space An organized list (or array) of numbers (or symbols) that graphically represents all possible non-overlapping outcomes of a probability experiment. (See Ready Reference 5)

Scale The regular intervals of the number line that are chosen to represent the full range of data on a graph.

Scatter plot A graph that shows a set of points (ordered pairs) based on two sets of measurement data plotted on a coordinate grid. (See Ready Reference 10)

Simulation Studying probability by collecting data on a model of an actual event.

Skewness A distribution is skewed if it has a long tail stretching out in one direction. The direction of the skewness is the direction in which the tail is pointing.

Split stem and leaf plot This is a variation of a stem and leaf plot. When a stem and leaf plot has a small number of digits on a stem, it does not present a good visual image of the distribution. The stem may be split to better identify patterns in the distribution. (See Ready Reference 8)

Stem and leaf plot A data display based on place value. It lists the greater place-value digits vertically (on the stem) and the lesser place-value digits horizontally (on the leaves) thus resembling the stem and leaves of a plant. (See Ready Reference 7)

GLOSSARY

Symmetry A distribution is symmetric if one half of the distribution looks like the mirror image of the other half.

Theoretical probability Determining the relative frequency of an event through mathematical reasoning.

Tree diagram A graphic representation that resembles the branching out of a tree. It is used to illustrate outcomes of an event. (See Ready Reference 5)

Trend An emerging pattern in the shape of the data display that can be seen on a scatter plot.

Upper extreme The largest value in the set of data.

Upper quartile When the data set is ordered from smallest to largest values, the data set can be divided into four quarters. The numerical value that cuts off the upper quarter of the data points is called the upper quartile. (Ready Reference 7)

Variable A quantity whose value may change or vary.

x-axis The horizontal axis on a coordinate grid.

y-axis The vertical axis on a coordinate grid.